THE PRICE TO PAY

Joseph Fadelle

THE PRICE TO PAY

A Muslim Risks All
to Follow Christ

Translated by
Michael J. Miller

IGNATIUS PRESS   SAN FRANCISCO

Original French edition:
Le prix à payer
©2010 by Les Éditions de l'Oeuvre, Paris

Cover art by Stephen Dudro

Cover design by Riz Boncan Marsella

CONTENTS

Introduction   7

I. Conversion   11
    Massoud   11
    The Call   33
    Solitude   47
    Fatwa   82
    The Trial   93
    A Sad Celebration   109

II. The Exodus   121
    "The Church Asks You to Leave"   121
    Secret Preparations   129
    Farewells   137
    In Exile   145
    Alarm   154
    Baptism   160
    "Zeal for Your House Will Consume Me"   169
    State of Grace   175
    Fratricide   183
    From One Flight to Another   195
    Respite   201
    Farewell to the Near East   204
    Viaticum   209
    "French, the Language of God"   215

Epilogue   221

INTRODUCTION

What then shall we say to this? If God is for us, who is against us? He who did not spare his own Son but gave him up for us all, will he not also give us all things with him? Who shall bring any charge against God's elect? It is God who justifies; who is to condemn? Is it Christ Jesus, who died, yes, who was raised from the dead, who is at the right hand of God, who indeed intercedes for us? Who shall separate us from the love of Christ? Shall tribulation, or distress, or persecution, or famine, or nakedness, or peril, or sword? As it is written, "For your sake we are being killed all the day long; we are regarded as sheep to be slaughtered." No, in all these things we are more than conquerors through him who loved us. For I am sure that neither death, nor life, nor angels, nor principalities, nor things present, nor things to come, nor powers, nor height, nor depth, nor anything else in all creation, will be able to separate us from the love of God in Christ Jesus our Lord. (Rom 8:31–39)

Amman, December 22, 2000

Your sickness is Christ, and there is no remedy. You can never be cured of it.

My uncle Karim pulled out a revolver and pointed it at my chest. I held my breath. Behind him, four of my brothers looked at me defiantly. We were alone in a desert valley.

Even at that moment I did not believe it. No! I did not want to believe that the members of my own family, including the uncle whom I had served faithfully in the past, could really intend to kill me. How did they come to hate me so much—me, their own blood, the one who had played with

7

them as a child and had been nourished by the same milk? I did not understand it.

I did not understand either why, of all people, Karim, my beloved uncle, was the one threatening me now—the man whose skin I had so often saved when he got into trouble with my uncompromising father, the head of the family clan.

Why? Why could my family not simply accept my new life? Why did they want at all costs to make me become one of them again?

Little by little I began to understand with dismay: they were willing to do anything to get me back—me, the heir of the Musawi tribe, the favorite. I recalled the beginning of that incredible scene.

Karim started by saying, "Your father is sick. He insists that you come back. He authorized me to tell you that he would like to forget the past, everything that has happened."

My brothers had not haggled about the promises made by my father: one simple little yes on my part, and once again I could have the house, the automobiles, and the revenues. In exchange, I had to forget the harm that they [the Christians] had done to me!

How could I forget? And it was not just a question of forgetting! It was a question of my faith.

"I cannot return to Iraq. I am baptized."

"Baptized? What is that ... ?!"

I had become a Christian; my life had changed. I could not go backward now. My name was no longer Muhammad. My old first name no longer meant anything to me. But I saw very well that they did not even understand what I was saying to them. For them there was only a problem that could easily be settled with money. Everything depended on the sum to be offered. But all of their attempts ran into a wall: I refused to become Muslim again. To them I was an apostate.

We had already spent three hours discussing it at the side of the desert road. We had not made an inch of progress; each one was still encamped on the position that he had taken up. I was psychologically drained by the questions from every side.

Suddenly the tone intensified. The aggression became palpable, menacing: "If you are not willing to come with us, someone will kill you. In any event your body will be repatriated. And your wife and children will die of hunger here; they will come back to their country on their own."

For a brief moment I forgot the distressing situation that I was in and attempted a vague interior smile tinged with sadness. How could that Shiite Iraqi imagine for one second that an Arab woman would manage to earn a living by her own efforts, without the help of a man?

In the absence of a counterargument, my uncle Karim's eyes showed hatred and his expression hardened.

"You must have undergone brainwashing", he remarked coldly.

I could tell that he too was at the end of his patience, that he did not want to talk anymore. An evil like this called for a radical remedy: Islamic law, Sharia.

"You know our law. You know that there is a fatwa against you. This fatwa orders us to kill you if you do not become a good Muslim again like us, like before!"

I felt nauseous. My stomach clenched into an even tighter knot. I knew what was going to happen. In recalling that death sentence, Karim was obliged to follow through or else be considered an unbeliever or, worse, a renegade. My last support had just slipped out from under my feet. Confronting the inevitable, I exploded: "If you want to kill me, go ahead! You came with weapons and used force, but I would like to use reason and speak with you. Read the Qur'an and then the Gospel, and after that we can have a real discussion. Anyway, I do not think that you really have the courage to shoot me!"

The wave of anger and fear had made me talk too fast. What did I have to gain from such provocative language, like the swagger of the man sentenced to death who defies the firing squad one last time? Maybe I thought that, being foreigners in that country, they would not dare to alert the nearby localities by the noise and thus risk being arrested.

The detonation was deafening, with endless repercussions in the valley. By what miracle had Karim not succeeded in hitting me? In the depths of my soul I heard something like a female voice that whispered to me, "*Ehroub.* Flee!" I did not try then to explain this strange occurrence but took to my heels and dashed off as though escaping from a brush fire.

As I ran I heard bullets whistling around me. There were certainly some aimed at me, and aimed to kill me, judging by the trajectories, which came very close to grazing me. The seconds seemed to pass like centuries, until I managed to get far enough away that I could no longer hear their voices.

Since I was still running and thinking of the last minute that I had left to live, I did not feel the pain caused by the bullet. I just noticed that my foot became airborne, as though propelled by an incredible force. When I realized what was happening, I was on the ground, in the mud, with the sensation of a hot liquid running along my leg. But since I was completely wet, I could not tell whether it was blood or mud. My last thought was to notice the silence that had fallen. The weapons had stopped, no doubt when they saw me fall. Then I lost consciousness.

I

CONVERSION

Massoud

Basra, Iraq, early 1987

It was cold. I left our large family house in Baghdad to go to the South, fully intending to move like greased lightning through the barracks where nothing impelled me except the chance decisions of an administration at war.

I was twenty-three years old and had no desire to serve for three years in active duty for miserable pay, and especially not for Saddam's regime, which was fully engaged in a deadly conflict with the young Islamic Republic of Iran. Before I left, my father, Fadel-Ali, gave me some reassuring instructions: "You keep an eye on the area and see whether there is a zone exposed to combat, and then you come back and give me your report so that I can have you exempted."

I was all the more touched by that paternal concern because I had seen him completely torn to pieces and overwhelmed by the death of my older brother Azhar in the Iranian bombardments. And yet my father had paid to have him stationed in a no-risk zone.

After that tragedy he had moved heaven and earth to spare me that; I was the apple of his eye, his designated successor, chosen from among his numerous descendants to head the tribe. And for a few years that strategy had proved to be effective. Thanks to his extensive power, my father started by falsifying my identity papers, setting the date of my birth ahead two years to gain a little time before the fateful call.

Then, once I had officially arrived at the age of eighteen, I never responded to a single order from the army to report for service, because my father made sure that the commanders of the garrison would keep quiet by dipping into his fortune so as to offer each of them a nice house. And to top it all off, he took on as a [business] partner a government official who supplied me each month with the famous permission vouchers, an indispensable "open sesame" to avoid unexpected checks by the police. In the six years since the war had started, every young man walking about freely in the street without a uniform was a potential deserter!

But one day the stratagem was rendered inoperable by the determination and zeal of the new man in charge of military assignments, who wanted to fight against fraud.

Never at a loss for ideas, my father then agreed to let me leave for Basra, in the South, but for the sole purpose of gathering information about the tribe to which the commander belonged, in the hope of finding a new arrangement and to have me removed from active duty.

At the hour of my departure, confident in that assurance and impressed by the power of my family throughout the country, I just took a few items for a journey that would not last long, two or three days at most. That was enough for a round trip in that region near the Persian Gulf.

On arriving at the camp, I was taken from one office to another, and I finally learned that I was assigned to an infantry regiment situated about twenty kilometers [12 miles] from Shatt al Arab, the river that marks the boundary with Iran. The barracks was indeed a stopover for those who are returning from the front, and that is also where the munitions are stockpiled. Therefore I was stationed back somewhat from the combat zone.

Not until nightfall did I finally manage to meet the commander. It was too late to leave again, and so I decided to put off to the next day my request for special treatment. After all, if my career as a soldier lasted only one short night instead of the three years required by the regime, then that made me a privileged person—a privilege that I considered altogether normal and deserved by my rank in society. I would therefore put up with the thrills of military life for a few hours. Thanks to this adventure I was counting on gleaning safely an epic account or two from the front, so as to boast to my family and friends.

At the commander's orders, the administrative officer of the regiment asked me to follow him, and he showed me to the same barracks room as someone named Massoud [i.e., the room where Massoud was staying].

Along the way I asked my guide about the man with whom I was going to spend the night. "He is a good man," he told me, "a farmer. He is forty-four years old, and he is Christian."

At those words I stopped short, as though hit over the head with a club. I felt that I was becoming very pale and listless, and I dropped my things and the mattress that I had under my arm. Then surprise gave way to fear and panic. Losing control of myself, I started shouting like a madman: "What? That is just not possible. What kind of a joke is that? Take me back to the officer. Do you think that I, a Musawi, am going to sleep with a Christian?"

Dread rushed in and deprived me of all reason. Where I come from, Christians are regarded as impure pariahs, as less than nothing, and you must avoid any dealings with them at all cost. In the Qur'an that I had recited every day since my earliest childhood, they are heretics who worship three gods.

I remembered the insult, one of the worst that there are: "face of a Christian". If you call an enemy that, you risk death. I knew this because my father had intervened one day to settle a conflict of that type.

Baffled by my outburst, the soldier nevertheless found this advice to calm me: "The commander is a young man; he lacks experience. If you balk, there is a chance that he won't understand the situation and will react badly. So just spend the night as planned, and tomorrow we will find another solution."

Still overcome by emotion, I gathered my wits somewhat, but the night ahead of me sounded like a real nightmare. I was afraid of being touched by that Christian, of having to speak to him, or even to share my meal with him. Never in my life had I imagined such a trial.

As I entered the little room, head down and legs trembling, I found myself face-to-face with a man in the prime of life who seemed rather quiet.

"Where do you come from?" he asked me pleasantly, curious to know who his new roommate was.

The question brought me back to familiar territory, on which I could rely. I regained then a bit of courage, raised my eyes, and fixed them firmly on those of my interlocutor: "I am an al-Sayid al-Musawi, from Baghdad, a family directly descended from the Prophet", I told him in an icy tone of voice, as though to indicate the social difference that separated us definitively.

That was a little arrogant, because officially I no longer had the right to sign the noble title of Sayid on my papers. That had been forbidden by Saddam—who was not from a noble family—as soon as he took power in Iraq.

But my words, which were intended to cut short the conversation, seemed to produce their effect. Massoud made no answer. In silence he slowly pushed his bed farther away, and only after finishing that task did he declare that he suffered from allergies and that therefore we could not eat together.

Calmed somewhat by these arrangements, I set up my encampment for the night, all the while keeping an eye on the stranger. After all, I said to myself as I stretched out on my mattress, he does not look so bad, this Massoud; he even seems to be rather well-mannered. Maybe ultimately Allah is sending me to convert him to Islam.

I could not say that I was a strong believer, but I was an observant Muslim. And every good Muslim has the duty to convert unbelievers, so as to gain the heavenly reward promised to the brave: those women with the siren charms, milk and honey in abundance. To tell the truth, it was not so much the reward that interested me, as the good reputation that it could win for me among my family and friends.

More dimly, I realized with astonishment that this desire to convert someone, which was quite new to me, brought me a real satisfaction and also a bit more confidence to face that night.

The following day we had two beds and two completely separate sets of cooking utensils in the room. In that barracks there was no canteen, and everyone had to prepare his own food.

During the next two days I constantly watched that guy Massoud with suspicion, without ever managing to find fault with him, though. I was even surprised not to be bothered by the odor, because in my family it was taken for granted that you can tell a Christian by his bad smell.

Here, nothing about that man's behavior fed my prejudices. I felt embarrassed, disconcerted. Gradually my initial dread toned down and gave way to another feeling that was still timid: I felt intrigued by that Christian, since it was the first time that I had seen one made of flesh and blood.

And so I let myself be won over by curiosity, encouraged by something indescribable and attractive that emanated from his personality. After a while I was finally reassured as to Massoud's peaceful intentions, and I became bold enough to exchange a few words with him.

Because my father was a major agricultural landowner, we talked about farming; he too owned a lot of land in the northern part of the country. I could not help being impressed by the man's knowledge and experience, since I had left school voluntarily at age fourteen, being little inclined to sit at a desk for long periods of time—especially since I saw no use to it, given that I had always been destined to follow in my father's footsteps.

But I can also recognize education when I see it. The more I listened to Massoud, the more I was obliged to admit that he expressed himself with a distinction and a facility that I did not possess. I found again in him what I had liked in the many novels I had read as an adolescent: the ability to tell stories, to nourish my imagination.

In short, I fell, without really defending myself, under the charm of that cultivated man, even envying him his way with words. Once captivated, I no longer had any intention whatsoever of going to see the commander to ask him to change my room assignment. My goal, at that moment, was to discover Massoud's secret and to make it my own. And I, in return, would teach him the Muslim faith.

Life in active duty is actually rather quiet and left me with a lot of free time. Of course, I had to take turns at guard duty, especially at night, but overall they did not give me that much to do. Therefore, apart from two or three hours of daytime activities, in which Massoud and I were in charge of putting the arms depot in order, the two of us spent most of our waking hours together, without mingling with the other soldiers.

And I was glad to have that time, because I appreciated more and more my discussions with my barracks roommate. Of course, for the moment we avoided sensitive topics, especially the subject of religion. But I was on the lookout for the right moment to convince him of the superiority of Islam.

By chance during one conversation I learned that Massoud was born in 1943. Therefore he should not have been enlisted; he was too old to be one of the recruits called up each year to feed Saddam Hussein's appetite for conquest. While waiting for the government to recognize its mistake, which can take a lot of time, he was champing at the bit, thinking about his four daughters, whom he planned to marry to Christians from his village, near Mosul.

As for me, like the rest of my family I did not have much more sympathy than he did for that iron regime that despised the Shiites, even though, basically, my father is a moderate, like any leading citizen. His rank as patriarch of a clan often led him to conduct business with his Shiite brothers as well as with the Sunnis, despite their historical antagonism.

But there was more. Even before the Sunni Saddam Hussein had gained a monopoly on power, the Baath Party had been conducting a reign of terror for almost twenty years by eliminating its opponents. My family had never accepted that.

I proudly explained to Massoud that I belonged to a rich family of noblemen, the al-Musawi, which is present in Lebanon, Iran, and Iraq.[1] Through my father I can trace a direct

---

[1] The ayatollah Khomeini in Iran and the sheikh Nasrallah in Lebanon are members of the Musawi family.

line to the imam Moussa al-Kazemi, whose name means "he who knows how to control his anger". He in turn is one of the descendants of Ali, the young cousin and son-in-law of Muhammad. To the Shiite way of thinking, he is just as important as the Prophet.

But very early on, this aristocratic ancestry weighed heavily on my shoulders, the moment my father designated me to succeed him when he would be too old to govern the clan. He chose me, although I was not the oldest, no doubt because he considered me as the wisest and most obedient of his ten boys. From then on, my father, who made demands on those around him as he did on himself, made me understand very clearly that I had to be worthy of that choice, exemplary, in his image.

Therefore I have no memory of a happy, carefree childhood with games, laughter, and foolish pranks. For me it was duty instead; very soon I kept company with adults in the big meeting room beside the house and therefore experienced a kind of boredom.

Nevertheless, my situation as the favorite son involved certain privileges, which I would not have renounced for anything in the world. For anyone within the tribe who wanted to address a request to my father, I was the unavoidable intermediary; they all were afraid of him, to the point of not daring to look him in the face. Indeed, very conscious of his role in society, my father presented a serious, authoritarian countenance, without allowing himself the least bit of relaxation.

In that he was different from his own father; my paternal grandfather certainly had the same dominating character, but he was also a pleasure-seeker, who loved life in large helpings. He died at the age of 109, asking to be married a fourth time while someone poured drops of water into his mouth and his son read from the Qur'an to him!

My father, then, had not inherited that appetite for pleasure—lucky for the grandchildren! But to me, Fadel-Ali al-Musawi was not an inaccessible man either. I felt that he had a lot of affection for me; he was very attentive and not stingy with his advice as he taught me his business. In return I made an effort to be like him and to live up to his expectations.

My father was very concerned about how others saw him, and so he cultivated his image as a worthy chief of the tribe. Wearing a white keffiyeh [headscarf] fastened by the black ring of the Shiites, he was clothed in an oriental tunic with an overhanging midlength beard, because it was a sin to shave.

Among the Musawi you have to give the appearance of being a pious family, even if in fact you practice your religion as a formality. Certainly, I read the Qur'an every day in my room, but for me it was mainly a matter of "pretending to pray", of playacting. My prayer did not require any real involvement of my heart, or even a deep understanding of the text.

Inside the grand, one-story, twelve-room house, I likewise enjoyed a place of honor, particularly when it came time to sit down at a meal. There was no question of starting to eat without me, even if I was late, which caused a lot of jealousy among my brothers. As for my sisters, they did not take meals with us anyway.

My mother, Hamidia al-Hashimi, who is also a descendant from the Prophet, is my father's fourth wife. He did not keep the first three because they were not able to give him children. But he made up for lost time with his present wife, my mother, who gave him a magnificent family, the source of pride for him: twenty offspring, ten boys and ten girls, without counting the miscarriages!

And despite her fatigue from those repeated pregnancies, Hamidia kept the upper hand in the family home. She knew how to establish indoors the power that she did not possess outside, in Muslim society. She supervised the kitchen and the laundry and gave orders to her seven daughters-in-law and unmarried sisters, sometimes even violently, to the point of striking them.

The men, my brothers, were not under that authority, thanks to their sex, which gave them power over all women, including their mother—except, of course, for the respect that each one of us still has for the woman who carried him for nine months and brought him into the world. With her, too, I shamelessly took advantage of my privileged situation. My mouth still waters when I remember the five delicious loaves baked specially by my mother at my request.

At the madrasah, the "public school" that taught the Qur'an, I had been first in the class until the age of fourteen, at least if you believe the rigmarole in the official bulletins. It is not entirely certain that this judgment was totally fair and impartial, inasmuch as my father, who once again was watching over everything, made some of the biggest financial contributions to the school! The principal himself came to the school in person to register my enrollment, an exceptional act merited by my special status and the importance of the al-Musawi.

At the start I really liked school; it was the only place where, as a child, I could play with other children. Then, when I was around thirteen or fourteen, school became for me a waste of time; it hampered my freedom and did nothing to assure me of a future. In a country at war such as Iraq, the regime encourages military careers much more than schooling and education. And for those who persevere, it is better to be a Sunni or to belong to the Baath Party in order to get a civil service job. That was not my situation, and so I counted more on paternal favors than on instruction to make my way in society.

For all that, my apprenticeship as future chief was far from intensive. I spent hours in that immense reception room where my father dealt with his business, when he was not traveling the country to settle disputes among tribes. For my brothers and me, then, the work consisted essentially in making sure that someone was on duty, so that the people could come for advice at any hour of the day.

Between visits, while my father's farmhands were hard at work on the land, my brothers and I used to have coffee in the grand hall while endlessly discussing the rain and the fair weather. Sometimes—this was a favorite distraction in our idleness—my father took us with him on his trips. I considered myself then as one of the most influential members of a governmental delegation.

But that did not happen often, leaving me therefore with long stretches of free time. There were very few possible leisure activities: we had only one television channel, Saddam Hussein's, because satellites were forbidden by the regime. So I took refuge in reading. I devoured everything that fell into my hands so as to satisfy my curiosity: novels featuring imams, books about history and medicine, and even some poetry.

What astonished me most about Massoud was above all his ability to listen to my story kindly, with extraordinary attention, although I was only twenty-five years old and, all told, had not seen very much of life. Although convinced of the superiority of my tribe, I did not have the calm assurance of that man which, it seems, only age and education give.

Three days later Massoud was away for the whole day on a mission. I found myself alone, walking in circles in that little, windowless room, like a lion in a cage. I felt unoccupied and without purpose.

After a while I started to inspect visually my roommate's corner and spied, on a shelf, a little book. As I approached to pick it up, I discovered a mysterious and promising title: *The Miracles of Jesus.* On the cover there was a photo of a smiling man surrounded by a luminous halo. I did not know this Jesus, but emboldened by the siren call of a good, distracting read, I took the book over to my bed and opened it to the first page, forgetting as I did so all my prejudices with regard to what Massoud represented.

Never before in my books had I ever heard about miracles, much less by someone named Jesus. Even in the Qur'an, or in the life of Muhammad, I remembered no allusion to that sort of phenomena. My curiosity was therefore at its peak and swept away without hesitation the scruples that might have arisen while reading about the scene of a wedding, in Cana of Galilee, where the wine flowed in waves.

Good Muslim that I was, I should have closed the book immediately so as not to be contaminated by the impurity of that inebriating drink. But at that precise moment, captivated by the intensity of my reading, the thought did not even occur to me. More than the events themselves, what attracted and intrigued me was the person of Jesus, which brought me a salutary joy, without my knowing exactly why.

When Massoud returned in the evening, I hesitated for a long time to speak to him about it, so as not to offend his sensitive nature, but above all because I felt vaguely at fault—I, who a few days earlier had wanted to set up an airtight partition between the two of us.

It must be that sleeping on it clarified the situation, or else that the passing hours only made my curiosity increase:

the next day I had a burning impatience to ask Massoud about this Jesus, who obsessed my imagination. I admitted my transgression, a bit ashamed. He looked at me, smiling sincerely, without one ounce of triumphant irony in his eyes.

Emboldened by that implicit encouragement, I dared to ask the question that had been tormenting me since the previous day: "Who is this Jesus that your book talks about?"

"He is Isa ibn Maryam, [Jesus] the son of Mary."

The answer was totally unexpected and incomprehensible to me. [The name] Isa I recognized; it appears in the Qur'an, among other [names of other] prophets who came before Muhammad. But I had never heard that he had another name, nor that this Jesus/Isa had performed such extraordinary miracles.

"That's normal", Massoud answered, shrugging his shoulders. "He was called Jesus for six hundred years, and then when Islam arrived he became Isa."

A bit disconcerted, I nevertheless took the opportunity to inquire a little further about the religion of my companion-in-arms, so as to be able to convince him of the superiority of Islam.

"Tell me, Massoud, do the Christians have a book like the Qur'an?"

I had a little plan in the back of my head. In my mind, if the answer was negative the man would be much easier to convert, since he would have nothing to set against the Qur'an, the revelation of Allah by which Muhammad was inspired.

"Of course", he retorted to my great disappointment. "We Christians have the Bible, which is made up of two books, the Old and the New Testaments."

It seemed that it was going to be more difficult than I had anticipated. But in my missionary zeal, I was not going to let myself be thrown off by such a little thing. After reflecting for a few moments I arrived at the conclusion that it was enough for me to become informed about that book of the Christians in order to remove all the remaining obstacles between Massoud and a recognition of the unquestionable value of Islam. But again cold water was poured on my enthusiasm.

"For now I will not bring you the Bible, in any case not right away", he said evasively. "First I will ask you a question, just one, and you will answer me sincerely."

Terribly disappointed by such a lack of cooperation on his part, I agreed feebly, raising my chin, without making a peep.

"Have you read the Qur'an?"

"I certainly have", I said vehemently. "Do you take me for an infidel, a bad Muslim?"

"But have you really read it?" Massoud insisted gently.

"I tell you that I have read it, and I even read the whole thing every year during Ramadan! There are thirty parts in the Qur'an, and Ramadan lasts thirty days."

"And you have understood the meaning of each word, of each verse?"

The question, which pierced me like a sharpened dart, threw me off-balance. Bright red with embarrassment, I found nothing to say in reply. He had hit a sore point. For the imams had always taught me that reading the Qur'an from start to finish was what would be rewarded on the Day of Judgment, much more than understanding the text. Thus deciphering a single letter enables you to advance in piety, to gain ten indulgences, even if you do not grasp the meaning of the whole word. By that reckoning, every Muslim is well assured of attaining paradise—no worries about that! By way of explanation, the religious leaders had told me that in any case the Qur'an is a very complicated book to interpret, and that that is why the imams pursue very advanced linguistic studies. At the time this reasoning by the clerics had satisfied my curiosity, and more insidiously had legitimized my very superficial practice of Islam. Therefore I did not really search any further, which would have disturbed my little religious comfort zone.

Seeing that I was so closemouthed, Massoud pressed his advantage and proposed a deal to me: "If you want me to bring you the Gospel, that's fine with me, but on one small condition: you will first reread the Qur'an while really trying with your intelligence to decipher the meaning of it; be honest with yourself and do not cheat."

I certainly was not expecting such a proposition when I broached the subject of religion with Massoud. There I was, stormed in my own stronghold, obliged, if I was to pursue my ambition of converting him, to start over and reexamine my own beliefs, while he had made no concession at all. So as not to be stuck in a position like that, I was ready to accept his challenge; my pride was stung and I was sure that I would be able to prove to my interlocutor the greatness of the Qur'an. Inshallah! [If Allah wills!]

A moment later I realized with some annoyance that in my impetuousness I had overlooked one little detail: thinking initially that I was leaving Baghdad for a round trip that would take a few days, I did not take the trouble to bring the copy of the Qur'an that I keep in my room. I would therefore have to wait patiently until my next leave, in twenty-eight days, to be exact. Allah would surely be able to wait!

Nonetheless I did not remain idle. In order to keep up my conquering spirit and to chip away a bit at the titanic job that awaited me, I assailed Massoud with questions about Christians and their customs. That way, when I was back home, I would find more quickly the right answers with which to convince him.

While pestered in this way and summoned to give an account of his religion, Massoud however remained very prudent and laconic in his answers, as though he were ill at ease, on the defensive. At no time did he put himself forward or speak about his personal faith. Oddly enough, it even seemed to me that he removed himself from the world of the Christians, from the world that he nevertheless belonged to and described to me very precisely, although coldly and almost mechanically.

I concluded from this, a bit hastily, that his strange reaction was a sign that his religion was inadequate for the long haul and that he himself was aware of it. The goal that I had set for myself was very definitely within reach.

Meanwhile, despite this, I noted with surprise that my knowledge about Christians was rather approximate, or else totally false, and was more along the lines of hearsay. One day, in my father's large reception room, I had heard that Christians gathered in their churches not to pray, as at the mosque, but rather to indulge in enormous orgies.

Patiently, therefore, Massoud set about explaining that inside the churches the priests say Mass, during which they consecrate bread and wine, which they call the Eucharist. All that ultimately left me rather indifferent. In any case, whether through cleverness on his part [or not], nothing that he said seemed to me to offend against either the Qur'an or Islam.

But on the other hand, what I remembered from his explanations and what utterly astounded me was to learn that among the Christians, the priests do not have the right to take a wife. That was something that seemed to me hard to believe, and, when you get down to basics, even absolutely impossible for a man, whether or not he is religious. For in

Islam, marriage is an obligation that is translated by the term *nikah*, which literally means "the sexual act".

Certainly this Christian religion was extremely bizarre, and it was very urgent that I pull this sympathetic man out of the error into which he had fallen!

Back in Baghdad on my first leave, I made use of the seven days that were granted me to elaborate my plan of action. First, I began with what ought to have been the end, namely, to buy a horse to welcome the new convert, as custom demands. I already imagined my triumphant arrival at my house, holding by the bridle the animal on which Massoud would be seated, dressed in white like the kings—what a trophy to bring back from the war!

Quite happy with anticipation, I said nothing to anybody about my plans, and everyone imagined that I was preparing some surprise or other, without daring to ask me about it. Then I arranged to isolate myself as much as possible for the rest of the week. I made only brief appearances in the large common room, abandoning the business of my father, who, at any rate, had gone on a trip. During meals, which I took as quickly as possible, I was anxious about only one thing: to return to my room, without taking any further interest in my friends or my brothers. In turn, they respected my relative isolation.

Therefore I had all the leisure I needed to immerse myself in the Qur'an, keeping in mind that I had promised Massoud to examine the text honestly. In doing that I also found myself, for the first time in my life, alone, confronting myself, without diversion or distraction, obliged to face candidly something that made up a large part of my identity: Islam.

That is where my troubles began. However, I should have been suspicious and listened to the advice, in a verse from the Qur'an, not to go deeper into something that could disturb your faith. But my pride was stronger than my caution, and I did not reject Massoud's challenge. And then, too, I had confidence in the strength of my religion.

As I opened to the first page of the sacred text, I did not doubt for one second that I would return unscathed from that scriptural voyage. The first lines of the Al-Fatiha, which serve as the prologue of the Qur'an, gave me no particular difficulty. It is the best-known prayer, the one that millions of Muslims recite every day.

But as soon as I got to the second sura [chapter], called "The Cow", or Al-Baqara, things got complicated. I stumbled on almost every verse, thoroughly perplexed, and my reading of it became extremely difficult and slow. Thus I did not understand why, verse after verse, Allah lowered himself to defining the rules for repudiating a wife and delaying one's prayers, and so many very procedural details that, to my mind, were without any real religious value.

Another discordant note for me was that I did not get the Qur'an's insistence on defining the superiority and authority of men over women, who were considered most of the time as inferiors, having half of the brain of a man, and sometimes impure, when they have their periods.

I realized that I had lived for all those years in the midst of segregation, accepting it, moreover, very well. But I had not realized that it came straight out of the Qur'an and its regulations. And in the depths of my conscience I was no longer quite sure that that was really in keeping with a law of love.

For instance, in verse 34 of the sura on women, An-Nisa, which orders a man to "admonish" those women "on whose part you fear ill will and nasty conduct", then to "leave them alone in beds" and, if need be, to "beat" them.

So as to get to the bottom of the matter, I took advantage of my leave to go consult Sheikh Ali Ayatla, a friend of the family who was also an ayatollah, in other words, a learned Shiite clergyman, considered as an expert on the subject of Islam. I submitted to him another verse that was difficult to swallow, which rules that women are the property of men: "Your women are a field for you to cultivate, so go to your field as you will" (sura 2:223). This means that men can do with them whatever they want, including sexually.

The sheikh's answer, to tell the truth, did not convince me. For him, and for the imams who have studied the question, it means that a man can make love anywhere, except at the mosque, at any time, except during Ramadan, and in any way.

Seeing my skeptical demeanor, the ayatollah, who was fond of me, advised me to immerse myself in the life of Muhammad and then to come back and see him. That would allow me, he said, to understand the Qur'an better. But again, I had to lower my expectations when I read that Muhammad married a seven-year-old girl, Aisha, or that after having married off his adoptive son, Zayd, he took his [Zayd's] wife, his own daughter-in-law, to make her his seventh wife. But for my imam, that explains why the Qur'an forbade adoption. As for me, I found that that was an odd way of demonstrating what is good or not, by taking the prophet Muhammad alternately as an example and a counterexample!

In short, after a few days of intense reflection, the Prophet's behavior and life became a source of embarrassment to me: all those problematic verses could not come from Allah. I even came to consider it a blasphemy to think that way. But despite all that, I did not call into question the suras of the Qur'an as a whole. I told myself that the rest must be completely in conformity with the idea that I had of a benevolent, merciful God.

On returning to Basra, I resumed military life and plunged again with even more interest into my critical examination of the Qur'an, without however informing Massoud of my doubts. For his part, he did not ask me too many questions. And that was very good.

Our everyday life was Spartan. We cooked on an oil stove and ate individually, sometimes at the same time, but without mentioning religion. It was as though a tacit agreement—his bashfulness, no doubt, and a mild anxiety on my part—prevented us from doing so.

The petty events of daily life were what embellished our conversations, especially the hazing by our superior, which I found very difficult to take, inasmuch as he was of humbler extraction than I.

Deep down, I was very upset that I had not found the certitudes of faith convincing. The following weeks left me depressed and increasingly turned in on myself, the more the foundations and the sacred things of Islam, which were my landmarks, collapsed one after the other.

I realized that the Qur'an had structured my life very thoroughly until then. If the sacred text of Islam had lost its persuasive force for me, to the point where I doubted that it was the word of Allah, then my whole life from then on seemed quite fragile to me.

Where was the sense of pride that I used to derive from my name, my family, and my illustrious heritage? On what could I base my life if Islam was no longer its pillar? Whom could I really believe from now on? I had lost all my initiative, given over to doubt as though I were wandering aimlessly in the desert, without any sign of what route to take.

As though by a survival instinct, I clung to the idea that perhaps the Qur'an had been compromised, altered. I felt a nameless anxiety, and my stomach clenched when I thought about what had become of my life.

Even the life of the prophet Muhammad, which previously had seemed full of glories and skill, was no longer a consolation to me. In my sadness I saw in it, on the contrary, a series of adulteries and thefts. How could that man be a man of God? How could I want to resemble him, when he had done the opposite of what he used to preach? How could he require a woman who lost her husband to wait three months and ten days before remarrying, when he himself had married a woman the same day on which she lost her husband, [who was] assassinated along with six hundred persons by the solicitude of the Prophet?

What reassured me somewhat, in my spiritual slump, was that despite everything, I continued to believe in Allah and in his goodness, which is greater than all my doubts, greater than the Qur'an itself or of Muhammad.

Depending on my mood, often in the evening I happened to stop for a long while to contemplate that magnificent region, with its crystalline rivers and sky, its sandy valleys surrounded by desert mountains. In watching the sunset, it seemed obvious to me that the local legend was right in claiming that the Garden of Eden was located in the Shatt al Arab.

And the view of that untouched, beautiful wilderness calmed my sadness for a moment, for I could not believe that nature was so beautiful and that there was no Creator.

And so, after three or four months of reflection, I found myself obliged, not without some bitterness, to acknowledge that my faith had been thoroughly shaken by this critical examination. If Allah existed, and I deeply believed that, I was nevertheless convinced from then on that no religion could arrive at the truth about that immense divine Being.

In those circumstances, I no longer had any chance of convincing Massoud, much less of converting him to Islam. Nor was I about to share my conclusions with him: for me that would mean defeat. The mere thought of admitting it to him, after having so boldly made a show of my confidence, filled me with embarrassment. As a worthy representative of the Musawi clan, like my father, I dreaded losing face.

And at that moment I experienced something even worse than dishonor: the shame of having gone astray like that, of having believed so tenaciously in what now seemed to me to be worthless nonsense, a scheme. I had been duped by some magic from which I found it difficult to recover.

To save myself from the total shipwreck of my self-esteem, I clung then to my one remaining hope: that of leading Massoud to the same conclusion that I had reached. If I could manage to persuade him, I told myself, that his own religion is a snare too, then we would once again be on equal footing, and then with complete peace of mind I could confide to him my own doubts about Islam.

That is the only way I could see of preserving the affection and esteem of that man, whom I had come to like so much as the days went by.

That being the case, for the moment I could not see the slightest opportunity for putting my resolution into effect. All in all my knowledge of Christianity was rather superficial, but more importantly in the depths of my heart I had a profound disdain for that religion. Although my belief in the Qur'an had been reduced to nothing, to me Christianity was still inferior to that nothing. Therefore I did not see how to answer Massoud, to show him the emptiness of his beliefs without offending him.

The Call

May 1987

That morning when I woke up I was in a singularly good mood, as though I had been cured of a long illness, specifically of the illness that had made my soul so languid throughout those past weeks.

I gladly breathed the spring air, which suited my joyful spirit at that moment, as the dry heat of the summer approached but was for the moment quite tolerable.

What made me so lighthearted was that for perhaps the first time in my life I remembered one of my dreams. That was something that had never happened to me throughout my childhood; this made me extremely jealous of my brothers and sisters, who in the morning all related their extravagant dreams! I never got to be one of those celebrities for a day, to whom we listened avidly, hanging on their every word, fascinated by the marvels of the imagination. I had developed such a grudge over it that I went to consult a doctor to make sure that I did not have some abnormal condition!

That morning, I finally had my revenge for all those years of fraternal humiliation: I had become like everyone else, capable of telling a dream, and not just any dream. How I wished that my brothers were there to be present at this exceptional event.

The dream, then—I remember it very clearly—situated me on the bank of a stream that was not very wide, not quite a meter [yard]. On the other bank was a figure about forty years old, rather tall, dressed in a beige one-piece garment in the Middle Eastern style, without a collar. And I felt irresistibly drawn toward that man, impelled by the desire to go over to the other side to meet him.

Then when I began to leap over the stream, I found myself suspended in the air for several minutes that seemed to me like an eternity. Somewhat alarmed, I even feared that I might never be able to come back down to earth.

As though he had sensed my growing uneasiness, the man on the other side stretched out his hand toward me, so as to help me cross the watercourse and land beside him. At that moment I was able to have a leisurely look at his face: blue-gray eyes, a thin beard, and medium-length hair. I was struck by his beauty.

Looking at me with an infinitely kind expression, the man slowly spoke to me a single enigmatic sentence, in a reassuring and inviting tone of voice: "To cross the stream, you must eat the bread of life."

When I awoke the next day, that incomprehensible sentence was nevertheless clearly engraved on my brain, while the charm of the dream in the night gradually wore off. Still overjoyed, in an almost childish way, about finally having had *one* dream of my own, with a smile on my face, I did not feel the need to try to understand the meaning of the mysterious words. That dream was my treasure, and that was enough to make me happy. Therefore I had no desire to know its real value.

When I opened my eyes, I was no longer alone in the barracks room. Massoud had returned from leave, and he greeted me calmly with his smiling eyes.

Then he held out to me a book with his rough, peasant hand. "Here is the Gospel", he said to me very simply. Five months after I had asked him for it, he remembered my request after all!

And he added right away, as though to anticipate my criticisms: "Do not worry if there are four different versions of the life of Christ. These four Gospels tell the story in four different ways."

It is true that for someone as uninformed as I was—a Muslim, moreover, who was accustomed to the one Qur'an—these distinct versions seemed to be an aberration. But that morning my mood was too impulsive to stop and linger over that detail. Besides, the Qur'an had lost its credibility, in my view. So I impatiently opened the book of the Christians and came upon the part entitled "Gospel according to Saint John".

"Begin instead with some other passage, the Gospel of Matthew, for example. It is easier to start with that", Massoud advised me over my shoulder.

By what mysterious plan did I not follow his advice while taking this book of the Christians over to my mattress? Defiance, stubbornness, the desire not to bend completely to the orders of a Christian, especially in religious matters? In following my own idea, I started my reading with the last version, the one by the author named John. Absorbed in my work, I even forgot to have breakfast and did not notice the passage of the hours.

When I got to chapter 6, I stopped short, dumbfounded, in the middle of a sentence. My brain was seething. For a second I thought that I was the victim of a hallucination, so I plunged again into my reading, at the precise place in the book where I had stopped. No doubt about it, I had not been mistaken.

By what miracle I cannot say, but at that moment I had just read the words "the bread of life", exactly the same words that I had heard several hours before in my dream.

To get to the bottom of it, I reread slowly the passage in which this Jesus speaks to his disciples after multiplying the loaves for the crowd and tells them, "I am the bread of life; he who comes to me shall not hunger" [Jn 6:35].

Then something extraordinary happened inside of me, like a raging fire that swept away everything in its path, accompanied by a sensation of well-being and warmth—as though all at once a dazzling light illumined my life in an entirely new way and gave it its full meaning. This is how I imagined a lightning strike, and it was even more than that!

I had the impression of being inebriated, while an extraordinarily strong feeling arose in my heart, almost a violent, amorous passion for this Jesus Christ about whom the Gospels speak.

At the same moment I understood that my dream the night before had been more than a dream: there had been in it, I sensed very clearly, something like a call or a personal message that was addressed to me through those words, by whom exactly I did not know; I was incapable of saying what that man meant to me, or what the significance of all this was.

All that I knew was the joy that event brought me. I was certain that from then on my life would never again be like before.

In the days that followed I had only one thing in mind: to prolong my inebriation, to feed it again by reading all four Gospels. I wanted to know everything about this Jesus—to be inspired by his way of life, to absorb every last word that he pronounced, to be indignant about what those people said about him.

And for the first time I had the impression that a breach was opening in my disdain for Christianity. The religion that I had considered as inferior appeared to me henceforth in another light. I vaguely sensed that it contained a pure source of love, of freedom—so many benefits that until then had been totally absent from my practice of religion.

Instead of the precepts and formal obligations, such as praying five times a day, the words of the Our Father in the Gospel resounded in my head and in my heart like a healing balm. If Allah speaks like a father who loves his children, if he pardons even the sinners, then my relation to him could no longer be the same. I was no longer in submission or in fear but rather in love, as though in a family.

Even repentance, which does exist in Islam, seemed to me to be liberated here from a load of conditions and duties that made it a heavy burden.

At that time everything that Islam had inculcated in me, that had shaped my personality and my thinking, was mixed up in my mind with this new way of looking at faith that, I must admit, I found extremely attractive.

And so I had in my head all the names of Allah given in the Qur'an. There are ninety-nine known names: Eternal, Unbegotten, One, Inaccessible, Firm, Invincible, Glorious, Wise, Benevolent, Merciful, but also Avenger.

And yet there is another name, the one hundredth, which no one knows. I had the impression that I had discovered that day this mysterious and unknown name of Allah: it is Love.

From then on the conquering spirit in me was completely calmed and I had no intention of converting Massoud. I had only one desire: to be able someday to eat this "bread of life" too, even though I did not understand exactly what it was.

Among all the new things that I was now encountering on the order of faith, there were some that contradicted my old convictions head-on—for instance, the status of Jesus: for the Christians, he is the Son of God, which is totally unthinkable for a Muslim. That would be tantamount to saying that Allah is married and has a wife! Despite my uncertainties in matters of religion, I was not ready to accept that. In my view, the Christians were wrong: Jesus was only a servant, an illustrious one, to be sure, but nothing but a servant of Allah.

To make sense of all this and to emerge from the confusion into which I had plunged, I saw no other solution this time but to open up to Massoud. I would therefore have to swallow my pride and admit to him that I had lost all confidence in Islam.

A bit sheepish, but at the same time thrilled to be able to communicate my joy, I took the trouble to tell him about the extraordinary adventure that I had just experienced, just a few days earlier.

Still carried by the first wave of enthusiasm, I savored the pleasure of announcing to him that from now on we shared more or less the same faith in Jesus. And above all, like a child who is preparing a gift in secret, I took delight ahead of time in the joy that I was going to bring him by this good news—at least that was what I imagined.

But it was not the anticipated smile that I saw appearing on Massoud's face. On the contrary: he went pale, his expression remained cold, his jaw clenched. Only the intense activity that I read in his eyes told me about the feelings that agitated him at that moment. What I saw was fear, a fear close to panic that shook the interior of that sturdy man.

Positively disarmed by his demeanor, I no longer understood it at all and looked at him inquisitively. For this change in him had taken place rudely, at the end of my story. At the beginning he had given me the impression, rather, that he was listening to me carefully, encouraging me by his kind attention.

I had said nothing extraordinary or especially daring, apart from the strangeness of my dream. I was just telling him my intention of announcing to my family my new faith in this Jesus Christ when Massoud exploded: "You do not realize! They will kill you."

I had never seen him like that. He was beside himself and seemed to have lost all self-control.

"But that is not possible! My family loves me; they cannot want to do me harm."

"Listen, I beg you", Massoud told me, changing his tone abruptly. "You are putting your life in danger, and mine with it. In this country you cannot change religion just like that. It is punishable by death!"

At that moment I had a flash of insight: I finally understood why at the beginning of our acquaintance Massoud had seemed so hesitant to speak to me about his faith, about his way of life. He knew the risks he was taking.

But still inflamed by my very recent reading of the tragic story of Jesus, I replied, "Christ died, too, and afterward his disciples faced great dangers in order to follow him. I read it in the passage that follows the Gospels: the Acts of the Apostles. Why shouldn't I do the same, after all, if I love Christ?"

"But Christ does not want you to die. If you really believe in him, then let's pray to his Spirit to enlighten us. And I beg you once more, calm your excitement, and swear to me that you will never speak about all this when you return to your family!"

I was not sure that I actually understood the reality of the danger that Massoud was talking about, but to tell the truth I really did not have a choice. If I wanted him to guide me along the path of faith, a path that still appeared to be obstructed by obstacles connected with what Islam had taught me, I was obliged to comply with his demand, since he was the only Christian I knew.

That is why I agreed, reluctantly, to cover with a veil of silence what would henceforth be, I could tell, the new driving force in my life.

During one of my subsequent leaves, despite everything, I dared to break that rule of silence, at least partially, by going to the ayatollah to submit one last question: this time about the Gospel of the Christians. What did he think about it?

His answer was that in this book there are things that are true and others that are false or that were omitted—for example, the arrival of the prophet Muhammad after Isa. It is also false to say that Isa is the Son of God.

Then the ayatollah concluded by asking me not to come to see him again. "Your questions", he told me, "are too difficult and too tiresome for me. Usually people come to consult me to find out what is a sin, haram, and what is not, halal, in their everyday lives. So put aside all these questions about theology; it is too complicated and it will do you no good."

That did not really enlighten me, but I had learned one thing at least: from then on it was useless to look any further for answers in my former faith, in Islam.

I was convinced that the last four months that I had to spend in the camp would be among the happiest of my young life. Does that explain why they also passed by at an incredible speed?

To all appearances, however, my life as a soldier continued strictly according to routine, in the dreary repetition of everyday tasks, although admittedly there were not many of them. A change had taken place inside of me, though, and also within the barracks room that I shared with Massoud.

What was new was that we two set about praying together, for hours at a time. Very quickly my companion taught me the sign of the cross as well as the usual prayers, the Our

Father and the Hail Mary, and how to meditate on the Gospel.

And so, with my guide, I discovered a closeness to Christ; I learned to speak interiorly with him, in a heart-to-heart conversation. For me that was a big change from the prayer in Islam, in which the essential thing that I had gotten from them was a respect for the ablutions [ritual washings], which are quite external.

Inside the barracks, all this took place in hushed tones, to avoid being discovered. That is why we often chose meal-times [to do so], when we ran less risk of being surprised by the other soldiers of the regiment. They were astonished to see that a Christian and a Muslim could spend so much time together, but that was all. Fortunately they were not so curious as to spy on us to find out what it was all about.

How surprised they would have been if they had known the subject of our long conversations, during which Massoud deployed all his knowledge to explain to me the mysteries of the faith. The Trinity, for example, is unthinkable in Islam. How can you make a Muslim understand that Christians have only one God and not three?

My companion went about it with simple images, drawn from commonsense peasant experience, so as to put his faith within my grasp.

"You see," he told me, "it is like the sun. There are three ways of perceiving it: you can look at it directly, or feel its heat, or you can see its reflection on the water."

I marveled at his skill in expressing himself about the things of God, and deep down, those difficult concepts of the faith were not really difficulties for me—because once I had read the Bible, I had believed in it spontaneously, naturally, as a child might have done, without asking myself too many questions. It appeared to me to be self-evident, even though I did take time seeking clarifications, so as to emerge from the confusion in my mind, which was troubled by all that I had learned before.

On the other hand, I was much more astonished to notice one day that my own way of looking at the people around me had changed imperceptibly. No longer was it the superiority due to my rank that governed my relations with the other soldiers but rather the desire to serve them, to love them as Christ surely loves them—even though, as far as I was concerned, I remained for the moment at the level of good intentions, without any effect whatsoever resulting from that fine sentiment!

In my family, likewise, I experienced with excitement that feeling which for me was quite new, that love of others which Christ commands in his Gospel. And then I had only one desire: to share with them the joy that dwelled within me, a joy that I had never known before!

However, during my next leave, faithful to the promise that I had made to Massoud, I allowed no sign of the fire that burned within me to appear. It was as painful as a repressed desire, and it was even more so when the time came for common prayer.

In my enthusiasm as a neophyte, I had indeed forgotten that little detail of family life, which was now extremely embarrassing for me: my father often received guests on business matters in the large common room, where everyone stood up to pray before starting the meeting.

This time I stood up at the same time as the rest of the group, automatically, thanks to deep-seated reflexes. But suddenly I realized what I was doing. I was overcome with confusion. With my fists clenched, my blood curdled at the thought that I was praying like a Muslim, whereas that religion no longer meant anything to me.

And yet, in my misfortune I was lucky: we did not pray aloud. It was enough, therefore, for me to pretend, to kneel down five times a day with the others, while reading the Fatiha [sura 1, central prayer of Islam] and sura 4 each time. But even that took a considerable amount of self-control to keep from running away, far, far away, from that pathetic comedy.

Occasionally, when I had the chance, I would avoid that troublesome obligation by pretending that I had something urgent to do or by absenting myself from the common room just before the prayer. But, alas, that was not always possible.

At the moment when the ritual began, therefore, I always had a brief moment of disgust, during which I saw myself playing a role: the role of a traitor—traitor to myself, because I was being unfaithful to my new faith, and traitor to my family also, because I was lying to them about the sincerity of my actions. In those moments I took a deep breath, so as to give myself the necessary courage—and prudence regained control of my emotions.

Fortunately the trial lasted only eight days, the duration of my leave, and then I could confide in Massoud. I hoped that he would relieve me of the heavy burden of the secret about my conversion. I broached the subject as soon as I returned: "I have a problem: I cannot continue to do this."

"To do what?"

"To pretend to pray like the rest of my family, as though nothing had happened! And then, in the Fatiha, which I am supposed to recite, the Qur'an mentions that those who have gone astray, in other words the Christians, cannot enter into the way of Allah."

Massoud reflected for several moments and suggested to me a solution: "During prayers you just have to call on Jesus in the depths of your heart. But above all," he insisted once again, "make sure that no one finds out anything. Otherwise you know what fate Sharia law reserves for the impious."

I knew it only too well, and if I happened to forget it, Massoud made it his duty to remind me of it at every opportunity. I began to think that he had no confidence in me, which ruffled my self-esteem a bit, unless he distrusted my ardor as a convert, and in that case I could only admit that he was right!

But Massoud knew men and the art of governing them. By dint of calling me to practice prudence and patience, the lesson finally sank in. On the good advice of my mentor, I agreed to commend myself to the Holy Spirit, who, he told me, is a good interior guide. I just had to ask him to show me the way to follow.

Yet Massoud was not content to soothe me with pious words. When he returned from a leave, he made a suggestion as to how I could stop leading this double life that would have been insufferable in the long run: "Listen, I have given a lot of thought to your situation. I even spoke about it to a priest in my village, and also to my own family. The best thing would be for you to come with me to my village in the North. You would just have to change your papers and have yourself registered as the son of my brother." And after a moment of silence, he added, shrewd peasant that he was, "You can marry one of my four daughters, whichever one you want. That way you will enter into the Christian community."

I smiled at that last proposition, thinking that, whether Christians or Muslims, there are still some things that all the inhabitants of this country automatically assume, for instance, that marriage is a family affair that is too serious to leave to the parties most interested!

But basically I was ready to do anything in order to become a Christian, even to get married, whereas until then the idea had not even occurred to me. What I wanted most in the world, the thing that attracted my thoughts and my will like a magnet, was baptism, and even more than baptism, sharing in the "bread of life".

The rest of it, the way of attaining that, was ultimately of little importance. Like a good pupil, nevertheless, I complied with Massoud's suggestion to invoke the Holy Spirit, so as to be guided along the right path—even though I was not necessarily convinced either that my friend's proposal was the best thing for me.

Thus the weeks passed by peacefully, following a rhythm of prayer times and discussions about the faith, which I pursued in fits and starts with Massoud. It would not have taken much to convince me to give up my next leave, had it not been for my affection for my relatives.

I dreaded above all having to lie again and to conceal my deep feelings. Nor did I look forward to refusing to answer my father again, who would not fail to ask me the name of the commander of the camp. Unlike him, I no longer had any intention at all of shortening my military service under those circumstances!

At the same time there was a great confidence within me: these last few months must have reassured him a bit as to the risks that I was running. Of course, the combat zone was not very far away, but nevertheless I was not on the front line, and the bombings never threatened the barracks where I was stationed.

When I returned to the camp, an unpleasant surprise awaited me: I found the barracks room empty. Not only was Massoud not there, but his things were also gone. Uneasy, I made a tour of the barracks, running and trying to understand what could have happened.

Out of breath, I finally learned from a soldier on guard duty that Massoud had left, abruptly discharged. So he must have received the famous letter that he had been waiting nine months for! That is the amount of time that the administration of the army would have taken to recognize its error in calling up Massoud and then to demobilize him from one day to the next. This occurs rather infrequently in the military, the experienced soldier told me, but it could be explained by the advanced age of the Christian.

It was a catastrophe. Massoud departed without leaving anything for me, not a word and no information. And I had been joyfully looking forward to seeing him again! I felt abandoned, almost betrayed, and to be quite honest, very much alone in facing the unknown that awaited me from then on.

I went back to my barracks room with my head hanging, suddenly feeling on my shoulders the full weight of the choice of life that I had made in abandoning Islam— not that I was questioning that decision for a moment; the joy of meeting Christ was still very real in me. But now that Massoud was gone, I began to gauge what it meant to swim against the current, in a familial and societal environment that does not accept religious differences.

In the days that followed I gave in to despondency and closed in on myself, as though prostrate and helpless. Even the prayers that I formulated without conviction became painful to me, because my heart was not in them.

And then suddenly, without my knowing why, the horizon cleared. Hope was reborn in the depths of my heart: no, it was not possible that Massoud had abandoned me like that! Not him. After all that we had been through together, the ties that united us were too strong. Although he had had to leave quickly, he would surely come back to visit me. He knew where I was and how much I needed him. He could not have forgotten me—it was only a question of time, time for him to make plans and to prepare for my arrival in his village. Having thus gotten a grip on myself again, I clung firmly to that idea, so as not to sink into despair.

Life regained its colors, but the days and the weeks went by too slowly in that stifling heat of the summer, without bringing me a single bit of news from Massoud.

At the end of a month I decided to tell my father the name of the commander, so that he could pull strings and have me exempted. That took only a few days, and then I went back to my family and home. At any rate, Massoud knew my name. He also knew my address in Baghdad. It was better for me to wait for him in my family [home] rather than in that dismal camp, where I no longer had any reason to stay.

Solitude

Baghdad, winter of 1987

Insidiously, doubt took hold of my mind. Several months had already passed since I had returned to my family's large home, and still no news from Massoud. Every day, every week that went by slowly diminished the hope that I had of seeing him reappear in my life.

And what if, ultimately, I had expected too much of that Christian? After all, he was the one who had advised me to be prudent. Maybe he had quite simply been afraid, afraid of the danger to his tranquility that I represented, afraid of putting his family at risk for a Shiite, even a convert, whom he had just met.

Reluctantly and slowly I resigned myself to the fact that I could no longer expect my old barracks roommate to save me. But what surprised me most was to discover that despite that disloyalty, I still had deep down a joyful confidence that adversities did not change. Curiously, everything happened as though my conversion had equipped me with a permanent resistance to anxiety and even to despair.

There was no lack of trials, however. Within a few months the ordinary life of the Musawi clan had become intolerable to me, because of the lies and the disappointments, like a poison infiltrating my veins drop by drop.

But I did not want to let it get me down. If I could no longer count on Massoud, I urgently had to find some other solution to escape from that iron collar that was strangling me,[2] now that I had realized the emptiness and meaninglessness of it.

When I stepped back a bit and reflected on it, was it Massoud who mattered most to me now or Christ? Was I waiting for Massoud and his friendship; was it a desire to recover our prayer life, that whole fraternal ambiance that we had experienced while we were so spiritually close for almost nine months? Or was what I hoped for most in the world something even beyond those ties that had been established and now were strained?

With a touch of mysticism mixed with fatalism, I ended up telling myself that if Massoud had been taken away from me it was surely for some higher purpose, that there was a meaning to all this, inshallah [God willing]. Maybe I was more attached to him than to the Christian religion, and from now on I would have to do without that crutch so as to deepen my faith.

After giving much thought to this for several months, I arrived at the conclusion that I absolutely had to take some action if I wanted to be able to continue living my newfound faith. If my old army buddy was not coming back,

---

[2] Cf. Ps 105[104]:18.

so be it! I had no other option than to find a solution
myself, so as finally to get out of that stifling situation—
all the more so, because with Massoud I had acquired a
taste for community prayer. I burned with the desire to
rediscover that atmosphere of the blessed months that we
had spent together! I realized also that alone my prayer
was very fragile, like a candle with a flickering flame—
certainly I still had with me that copy of the Gospels,
but that was not enough to nourish me. In my newborn
faith I needed to be strengthened by the fervor of other
believers.

To my mind it was simple enough: I just had to go knock
on the door of the churches in Baghdad and ask to be baptized. I even imagined that I would be received with open
arms, and with honors for my act of bravery—except that
in practice it was a bit more complicated. First I had to
manage to distance myself from my family for the time
required for a round-trip of around twenty kilometers [12
miles] to the center of the city. Sure, I had large intervals of
free time, but there was just one thing: I was afraid of arousing suspicions about my activities.

Prudently, I tried to space as much as possible these escapes.
I took advantage of the times when my father was traveling, when each of us was a little more on his own, delivered from the iron discipline of the head of the Musawi
clan. Indeed, when he was in the house it was difficult to
elude his eagle eye. He saw everything, was attentive to the
slightest detail, and made sure that everyone was busy at
some common task.

So it happened that several weeks passed without my managing to get free. When finally an occasion presented itself, I
seized it without hesitating, emboldened by the long wait. Each
time, alas, my impatient hopes turned to disappointment.

With each new attempt I had high hopes, which were in vain, for I soon came up short. Most times I found the door closed, or, more precisely, I was the one who made them show me the door of the church!

At the beginning I would push open the door of the church building without asking permission, hoping to be welcomed warmly like the prodigal son. Very quickly I had to change my tune, being scrutinized from head to foot by faces that were expressionless, even hostile.

After having weathered several refusals, I quickly understood. I was dealing with little communities in which everyone knew each other. Consequently, I was tagged quickly enough as a stranger, someone they suspected of coming to spy on the Christians, who were a very small minority in that country.

Since that approach failed, from then on I played the candor card: upon entering a church, I methodically sought to speak to the priest to ask him for permission to stay for a moment in that sacred place. It was more proper but hardly any more effective.

Here, too, I most often ran into a wall. "When you are Christian you remain Christian, and it's the same with Islam!" they would reply coldly when I announced my intention to ask for baptism.

One fine day, worn out by those fruitless comings and goings, by the stratagems that I was employing, by my double life in the bosom of my own family, I let my anger explode in the face of the poor clergyman who, like the previous ones, had just refused me unceremoniously:

"In the name of Christ, do you dare to put me out?!"

My reaction left him aghast.

"We have orders", he ventured timidly by way of explanation. "We cannot allow Muslims to enter our churches."

"And you cannot make an exception just once? Ask your chief, and make sure to tell him that this is at least the tenth church that has slammed the door in my face!"

Touched, no doubt, by my outburst, which must have seemed to him sincere, the priest promised to do so. He would present the question to the patriarch who supervises everything concerning the life of the Christians here in Baghdad, and in all of Iraq.

I took that promise as an opportunity that I could not miss, perhaps the only one, since I was not sure that there would ever be another. And so I declared to him my firm resolution to return to his church in a few weeks to hear the patriarch's answer.

During the days that elapsed after that new attempt, my morale was not at its highest: my enthusiasm was to a great extent dampened by my failures and I found myself reduced to calculating my chances of being heard, without really daring to believe it. From one day to the next my heart wavered, alternating between skepticism and timid hope, which was based on one slim certitude: that I had shaken the general distrust of those Christians by telling my story with all the ardor of my newborn faith. Would that be enough?

Several weeks later the prelate's decision, as it was reported to me, fell like the blade of a guillotine: "Sacrificing the whole flock to save one sheep is out of the question."

It made me sick. There I was, pounding on the Christians' door for months, and they invariably refused to let me enter their community out of a lack of courage that did not seem very evangelical to me.

But I also discovered that they ran enormous risks. As this priest explained to me, more comprehensively than the others, even under the secular regime of Saddam, welcoming a Muslim into a church can make it liable to the accusation of proselytism. And in Iraq, proselytism means death, for the one who practices it as well as for the Muslim who listens to him.

I understood these reasons, but in the depths of my soul, burning inside with a mad spiritual love, I could not help thinking of that Christ, who had no fear of risking his life to announce salvation to mankind.

Nevertheless, there was the result. I despaired of ever surmounting that wall that was set up between my desire for baptism and the people of the Church: they alone could manage it, but they refused. In a final challenge to fate, I made a resolution to speak to that patriarch myself. Maybe he would have less fear of opening the door of the Church to me.

His own door was not easy to find: I had a lot of trouble hunting down the headquarters of the patriarchate, which was very discreet in that administrative district. Every time that I showed up there, they invariably told me that His Beatitude was on a visit in Baghdad or else traveling in Iraq!

While waiting to track him down—and I doubted more and more that that would ever happen—I set about wandering like a troubled soul in the Christian districts, in the southern part of the city. I had the slim hope of entering into a relationship with the groups of Christians externally, even though I could not enter inside their buildings.

Alas, my perseverance went largely unrewarded. When by luck I managed to make contact, the conversation was cut short very quickly. All I had to do was pronounce the word "Muslim" to put an end to the exchange, even when I had announced my intention to become a Christian. And as for suggesting a further meeting, it was pointless even to think of it!

From one disappointment to the next, the months turned into years, without my making an inch of progress in my search for a Christian community. During that time, my sole refuge remained the Bible that Massoud had given me, his farewell gift, so to speak, which I had treasured.

I devoured the sacred book in hiding and thus spent long hours enclosed in my solitude, feeding on that Word which, alone, kept alive my desire for the "bread of life".

During my reading I very often found material that expressed what I was experiencing, even though those passages had been written millennia ago. In particular I liked very much the psalms of King David, with their alternating consolations and desolations. These texts reminded me of my successive states of soul during my wanderings in the Christian districts of Baghdad, recalling my growing passion for Christ but also the unacknowledged temptation of abandoning my investigations.

Even the phrases in the Gospel seemed to have been written for me, to invite me to hope: "Blessed are you when men revile you and persecute you and utter all kinds of evil against you falsely on my account. Rejoice and be glad, for your reward is great in heaven, for so men persecuted the prophets who were before you" (Mt 5:11–12).

What also prevented me from sinking totally into discouragement was Massoud, paradoxically. I still had in mind his warnings: "A Muslim is fated to meet many obstacles when he tries to join a Christian community in Iraq", he had cautioned me. Thanks to Massoud, I had also admired the courage of the first Christians and read the account of their persecutions.

That is why, despite the evidence, I resolved not to fall into despair. Everything that I encountered, such as refusal, rejection, and persecution, ended up reinforcing my faith and confirming that I was on the right path. In my extreme desire to encounter Christ, I had almost reached the point of experiencing a certain joy in suffering that way for his sake.

Finally, there was prayer, nourished by my readings and by the memory of the holy martyrs. I made an effort to pray conscientiously; without it, it seems that I never could have held fast.

In those moments when my prayer was empty, when I had nothing left to convince me to continue, it was also the passionate, throbbing voice of Oum Kalsoum, the Egyptian female singer, that was able to move me and restore my courage. Alone in my car on the way to downtown Baghdad, I happened to sing aloud, with a tear in my eye, the words of the love song "Aghadan Alqak", "Tomorrow I will find you again". Just pronouncing those upsetting words, I got gooseflesh. When I spoke them they expressed a genuine religious passion, which overwhelmed me much more than a purely human sentiment of love, of which I had never had the least experience.

As for my father, he would have liked me to be more interested in it, or at least to think of marrying. Several times during the four years that had elapsed since my return from the army, he had made some allusions to it, without insisting. But I saw very well that that made him unhappy, that all my brothers were getting married one after the other, whereas his favorite son remained single. If I was to take the reins of the Musawi clan someday, that was all the more reason that I had to have a wife worthy of that name.

What my father did not know was that, for my part, I had only one thing in mind: to leave home as soon as possible, so as to be able to live my faith in the daylight. I felt no desire to start a family here, to succeed my father as the new head of the clan, even though I would thereby acquire absolute power over my family, accompanied by countless privileges and riches.

At the beginning of 1992, therefore, I had no idea what was awaiting me when I went to the large meeting room just before breakfast, summoned by my father:

"My son, I have big news to tell you: I have found a fiancée for you!"

Stunned, I stammered an objection, having trouble articulating words:

"But . . . I really don't want to get married just now."

"Tch! At any rate I have already paid the dowry, *al-mahr*, and most importantly I have given my word to the family; therefore my own honor is at stake now. It is out of the question that you should refuse!"

So I was cornered, with no possibility of escape. If I backed out, it would be considered an insult to the bride's family and would surely provoke a serious conflict between the two clans. On the other hand, it was absolutely unthinkable that I could admit to my father the real reason why I did not want to marry!

Seeing my loss of composure, my father added, with the hint of a smile that was supposed to convince me, "Listen, I chose this wife for you because it is good for the family, but if you want to take another one, do what you like! You will just have to take this one like a piece of furniture in your room."

To conclude the discussion, he explained, in an imperious tone, that he had already made all the arrangements: I had been officially engaged for a month; the two families had reached an agreement, without any thought of informing us, my fiancée and me!

On that occasion, my father proudly related to me, they offered a profusion of jewelry and cosmetics, in keeping with tradition, so that the bride would be beautiful on the wedding day—which would take place in a week!

Pale with rage, but powerless, I had no alternative but to go along with this parody of a marriage. During the few days before the event, I watched as a spectator, joylessly, the preparations for the celebration where I would be at the center of attention. I felt a sadness that would have broken a heart of stone, walled up in my solitude without being able to confide in anyone. To make matters worse, I did not even have permission to see what my future wife looked like!

When the day arrived, they led me, like a robot, first to the Sunnis who staff the civil courts. That was where I first saw my future wife, Anwar, a beautiful, smiling, twenty-four-year-old woman, with black eyes and hair.

She seemed very timid, not daring to raise her eyes to look at me. Anwar seemed troubled also by the questions from the judge of the Qur'anic court, who asked her in downright vulgar terms whether she accepted the sexual act in order to establish the marriage contract. The bride became quite red. I was embarrassed for her. She hesitated to answer, to the point where the judge considered himself obliged to repeat his question. Her embarrassment increased, and a yes full of shame finally emerged from her mouth.

Then we went to see the sheikh, as Shiite tradition demands. The religious ceremony, *al-Zaffah*, took place in north Baghdad, in the great mausoleum of the imam Moussa al-Khadim, the seventh of the twelve imams venerated by the Shiites, and the seventh-century founder of my great family line.

The bride, adorned with jewels and dressed in white, was then escorted amidst festive brouhahas by a large cortege of sisters, aunts, and female cousins to the Musawi estate. The men, her brothers, remained at home to signify that their sister's marriage was a day of shame for them, since a man would take sexual possession of their sister.

During the grand social reception that followed, everybody came to congratulate the father of the groom, the great lord of the manor and the only real king of the celebration.

By chance during a conversation I learned that there was already a tie between our two families: one of my maternal uncles, then deceased, had married one of Anwar's six sisters who was much older than she. During the funeral of her brother, my mother noticed that young woman, whom she liked. Right away she saw in her the suitable wife that I required. Both my parents despaired of ever seeing me married, whereas all my younger brothers already were. This became for them an urgent matter.

Thus the first request had been made by my mother to Anwar's mother. The latter had been a widow since the death of her husband after a bout of indigestion due to a large meal one evening during Ramadan.

The request was approved, but that's only half the story. From the age of five, Anwar had been reserved for a sayid, a Muslim nobleman. This was a promise made by her mother after the daughter was miraculously saved from a house fire. As a result of this engagement, many suitors who asked for Anwar's hand in marriage were turned down, among them her cousin, who was madly in love with her. According to tradition, he had priority over the stranger. But he was not a sayid.

Wearing a wan, fixed smile, I did not consider my good fortune and endured that day fatalistically, without even having the consolation of looking at my wife, who was away from the wedding party with the other women. No one had asked her opinion either, I said to myself bitterly, neither her mother nor her brother who had taken charge of the family after his father's death.

After the guests had left, when I caught up with her, I asked her whether she was tired, whether everything was all right. She said that she was uneasy about facing the unknown in this new life, but she seemed somewhat reassured by this first contact of ours. Her big sister, she told me, had already described me as a handsome, kind man who was very well situated socially and religiously and, as everyone knew, had a fortune—in a word, what is called a good match.

Even though I made an effort to be considerate, I did not have much in common with Anwar—especially not my faith, the only thing that I was really concerned about now. I also realized dejectedly that from now on my search for a receptive church would be singularly complicated.

Indeed, my life as a newlywed required me to be doubly prudent when I decided to go on an expedition in Baghdad, or even to read the Bible. I quickly understood that Islam meant a lot to my wife. She wore a burqa [loose garment covering the face and body], and therefore there was a danger that she might denounce me to her family if she ever became suspicious of my absences or inquired about the book in which I was so often immersed.

So as not to arouse any doubts, I compelled myself therefore to attend family prayers from time to time, even though it was burdensome to me. For the moment we were living in my father's big house, but as the weeks passed I realized that I was not going to be able to keep my secret for very long from my family or from my own wife. I would have to find a solution so as to regain some freedom of movement.

It was the birth of my son, Azhar, less than a year later, on December 25, that gave me the idea.

I seized the opportunity of this blessed event, and I took my courage into my hands to go see my father. I supposed that he would be in the best possible disposition, rejoicing in the arrival of a male descendant who would perpetuate his line.

"You know, this birth changes a lot of things for me", I said gently as an opening gambit. "I myself would like to provide for the needs of my own family; I do not want to keep living at your expense, like my brothers who do nothing all day long. I have to have a separate home for the three of us. Let me go and buy a house. If necessary, I will work."

As I had foreseen, my father's first impulse was to refuse. It was so difficult for him to see part of his progeny escape from his control.

However, spurred on no doubt by necessity, I surprised myself with my persistence. I did not let myself be put off by his protestations. I knew that he loved me, that he had confidence in me. Then, given my repeated insistence, my father gave in, battle weary, to some extent so as to have peace in the family, but to some extent also because he had an idea in the back of his head. Indeed, he had noticed a little house down the road that he could buy up at a good price and that he wanted to give me as a gift. Thus he could still have the feeling that he was not losing anything, and at the same time, he was enlarging his estate.

Moving into our new lodgings nevertheless gave me more peace of mind with which to resume my explorations among the Christians. For I had not totally lost hope; above all, I did not see how I could continue to live much longer in that semiclandestine state.

Indeed, I had no choice; I had to bring matters to a head and find some way of living out my faith in the daylight, even if that meant abandoning my wife. That, at any rate, was the plan that I had devised before the birth of my son. From then on I was no longer so convinced of the wisdom of that plan.

Summer of 1993

By dint of patrolling far and wide the districts of Baghdad in search of churches, I began to be well acquainted with the Christian localities. Although the big cathedral in the old city seemed a bit isolated beside the immense souk [marketplace], the more recent districts in the South and the Southeast had been gradually settled by Christians who were more well-to-do, drawn by the quieter, more pleasant living conditions, whereas the Muslims had regrouped toward the North.

That is why I concentrated my investigations more and more in the Dora [also al-Dura, or ad-Durah] district, south of the old city, in which a majority of the population was Christian.

One day, parched after an hour of walking in circles through the dusty streets, I made my way by chance into a shop to buy a drink to quench my thirst. In that little supermarket where they sold a bit of everything, I immediately noticed a little icon of the Virgin Mary hanging on the wall behind the vendor. He was a young man, around thirty years old. I struck up a conversation, encouraged by the presence of that visible sign of belonging to the Christian community.

"Here it is rare to see that sort of religious image in the stores", I said to him, pointing with my chin to the icon. "That is a very beautiful portrait of the Virgin."

While looking at the price of the bottle that I was handing him, the man answered me by shaking his head,[3] without adding a word. Despite this, I left his shop with the feeling that there may be in it, after all, a more serious lead than I had found before.

---

[3] Shaking your head means no to Iraqis.

During the months and years that my investigations had lasted, I had never encountered such a calm affirmation of the Christian faith. Certainly, an image of the Virgin was less likely to offend the conscience of a Muslim than the cross, which you find on top of the churches and which therefore symbolizes the Christian religion. But even in that predominantly Christian district I had not failed to notice that the merchants generally did not advertise their religious preference, no doubt so as not to compromise their business.

On my return trip I had in the depths of my heart something like a gust of hope that suddenly eased the weight of my misfortunes. Impatient, I had only one desire: to return there the next day, at opening time. A deep-seated reflex of prudence, however, dissuaded me from doing that. Upon arriving home I promised [myself] nevertheless to go back as soon as possible to the shop of that brave man so as to try to befriend him.

It was a good inspiration. By the fourth visit the merchant cheered up and smiled at me. I made progress in my approach.

Each time, I tried to set him a little more at ease by showing him by my remarks that I too adhered to the Christian faith. By now I knew his first name, Michael; I knew that his family lived in Mosul and that he lived alone in a little house adjoining the shop.

This information did not fall on deaf ears. Here was the one who would facilitate my approach, since nobody would come to interrupt our conversations! The next time, therefore, I arranged to arrive in the late morning, just before lunch, with two pieces of meat to share with him. He accepted my gift without too much difficulty, inviting me into his house. Although externally composed, I was jubilant inside, because I could tell by his approving glance that I had done right in bringing pork.

In order to increase my chances, I had taken every precaution, to the point of choosing the meat of an animal that is impure in Islam. By that detail I managed to win Michael's confidence. From now on, I sensed, he would be ready to hear my story.

During the meal the presence of a crucifix in the main room supplied me with the opportunity to broach the only subject that I really had at heart: the faith.

Michael began by explaining to me that he preferred to put the Blessed Virgin Mary rather than the cross in his store, because it can happen that the latter provokes violent reactions among Muslims: they spit on the ground in disgust or insult the merchant. That is why, he explained to me, most crucifixes are found inside the houses of Christians, and not at their workplaces.

"Now I understand better", I exclaimed in a lively tone, "why I have met with so much hostility from Christians!"

"What do you mean?" he asked, intrigued.

As I finished telling him the story of my conversion and the long quest that followed, I confided to him what was now my greatest desire: to enter a church and to share in the bread of life!

"I beg you, come with me to one of the churches in the district", I urged him with my hands clasped. "You are known in the parish, and if I come with you I would surely have a greater chance of being accepted."

From the corner of my eye, trembling, I watched Michael's reaction. Until now he had listened to me without interrupting; he proved to be open-minded and seemed to sympathize with my trials. But as I had feared, he scowled at that last proposal; it was risky for him. In one sense I understood him perfectly: if ever the police came and caught him bringing a Muslim into a church, it was certain death, for him as well as for me.

But he did not say no. Too upset by the thought that he might completely dash my hopes, I left him abruptly, telling him that I would come by again soon to ask after him. And, I added to myself, to give him time to reflect.

In fact it was Michael himself who called me, a few days later, to suggest that I accompany him to Mass the following Sunday, at the church of Saint Basil. After setting down the receiver I remained motionless for a few moments, filled with a calm, wordless joy, astonished to see an opening appear suddenly on a horizon that until now had been so tragically blocked. Finally my efforts were bearing fruit.

If I had not been afraid of attracting my wife's attention, I would have fallen to my knees to thank the One who now occupied all my thoughts.

In returning to my activities, I felt that I was coming down with a fever at the thought that for the first time I was going to be present during Mass at the true sacrifice of Jesus, immolated for the love of mankind. In my overexcited mind, which was now working at full speed, I had already moved on to the next stage of my plan, which was to get permission from Michael to go with him to church every Sunday.

The following Sunday I understood nothing: all the words were spoken in Aramaic, a language quite different from Arabic. Despite that, I felt in that assembly an indescribable spiritual atmosphere that warmed my heart and consoled me in my misery. I felt that I was being carried by the community as a whole, which was something new to me.

Unfortunately for me, the Christian merchant did not practice his faith very regularly. From time to time he "forgot" the Sunday precept, opening his shop and conducting his business. For on Friday, the day of prayer for Muslims, clients were rare. Therefore he could hardly do without opening the store occasionally on a Sunday so as to pay his bills at the end of the month.

When I begged him not to abandon me while I was making such good progress, Michael suggested an alternative: he would speak about it to the parish priest, Father Koder. If the latter officially agreed to let me come to church, the merchant would then no longer need to chaperone me.

During the same week, coincidentally, a roadblock fell with respect to the patriarchate also. I had insisted on laying siege to that modern, very ordinary building, with no external sign to identify it, and this time the porter recognized me, closed the door, and disappeared for a few minutes. Then he opened it wide and stepped aside to let me in. He quickly told me that I would be received, not by the patriarch, but by his auxiliary, Bishop Ignatius Shouha [also Shuha or Shukha].

Very impressed, I was brought into a large parlor where the hierarch, in a cassock, was already sitting calmly on a gilded, sculpted seat.

Without knowing the reason for my impromptu visit, he sized me up with his glance and asked me my name, no doubt thinking that he was dealing with a Christian whose importance would be indicated by his surname.

The question caught me unawares and paralyzed me. I had carefully prepared a short presentation of my story, and here I was forced to rush headlong into my explanation, beginning at the end, without having time to prepare my interlocutor. I found myself speechless for several seconds that seemed to me interminable. Then, realizing how ridiculous my situation was, I was inspired and plunged in: "My name is Muhammad, I am a Muslim, and I believe in Christ. I want to be baptized!"

In pronouncing those words, I had the curious sensation of throwing myself off a cliff. The prelate jumped up from his chair, red with anger, as though jolted by an electrical charge. To my great surprise he seemed to lose his composure and then rushed toward me, shouting, "Out, out!" and pushed me unceremoniously toward the exit.

When I heard the dry click of the door closing behind my back, without a word, my legs no longer supported me and I fell down in tears on the street, shocked and overwhelmed by that totally unforeseeable violence.

The most difficult thing to accept was that that reaction came from the clergy, from one of its highest-ranking members; moreover, my dearest desire was to become a part of that same community of believers which is the Church! And to think that on the other side, in my family, I was considered a prince, destined to succeed the king. If it had not been tragic, it would almost have been laughable. But that inheritance meant nothing to me now: it would impose on me a religion that was utterly worthless in my view.

Sitting on the ground, I was annihilated. I no longer felt that I had the least bit of energy or resilience with which to face this discouragement, which completely overwhelmed me in uncontrollable waves. I remained there prostrate for several minutes until, meeting the inquisitive and sometimes disapproving looks of the passersby, I decided to get up and head back to my car.

On the return trip my thoughts were empty. In the rearview mirror my face no longer had any expression. My hands stiffened on the steering wheel, and I clung somehow or other to the only idea that still comforted me a little in my confusion: "If it is the will of God ..." Ultimately, perhaps, my place was not there, in the middle of

the Christian community, but rather on the margins, and I
was destined to live out my faith alone and in secret.

When I arrived home, I must have seemed disconcerted.
My wife, Anwar, paused a moment to look at me, with a
question in her eyes. But since I had routinely responded
to her questions with monosyllabic answers and stony silence,
she said nothing. She finally told me about a call earlier in
the day from someone named Michael. I immediately
grabbed the phone, prompted by the intuition that fate was
perhaps not so unjust—and I was not mistaken!

The Christian told me excitedly that the parish priest,
Father Koder, agreed on his recommendation to see me at
his house, that same evening. Surely it must be written somewhere that the love of Christ leads those who follow him
through great trials, but also intense joys!

A few hours later, therefore, I again took the steering wheel.
My wife did not ask me for any explanations, yet I sensed that
she was intrigued by these regular comings and goings. For
the moment the meeting that evening was what occupied my
mind, along with the still-searing memory of my encounter
with the auxiliary bishop to temper my rekindled hope.

My fears vanished the moment I first contacted that simple
priest in a cassock. The man who welcomed me by offering
me a cup of tea was a tall man, around forty years old, with a
strong personality, according to Michael, but very charis-
matic. Upon my arrival I sensed that he was rather nervous.

Nevertheless, when I told him, during the course of our
conversation, that I was married, I saw very clearly that he
relaxed, that his natural misgivings with regard to me were
dispelled.

"It very often happens", he explained to me with a smile,
"that Muslims ask for baptism for an altogether prosaic reason, so as to be able to marry a Christian woman."

My married status therefore reassured him about my intentions. He was now eager, he told me, to hear the story of my conversion in detail, after the brief summary that Michael had given him. Now I was more at ease.

As I told my story, I understood from the friendly nods of his head that he followed what I was saying, that he took me seriously and would not reject me again. I relaxed: finally I felt that I was understood by a clergyman. It was an immense relief, as though an enormous weight had been taken away from me, the fear of being the only person to believe in the call that I had received.

I was not even sure that Father Koder really gauged the extraordinary impact of his words when he concluded, after listening without once interrupting me, "I am convinced that your faith is sincere. Therefore you can come to the parish when you want."

Those words flowed into me like honey. It was a soothing balm poured over six years of rejection, perseverance, and hopes that were renewed and regularly disappointed. With this priest it was as though the great Church, whose contours I did not yet see clearly, was now ratifying my faith experience, was declaring it authentic, and was symbolically opening up its doors to me by this "open sesame", his offer to let me enter into his little parish church.

Baghdad, 1994

Thus I learned during that momentous evening another bit of extremely important information: my marriage was a guarantee of authenticity in my faith journey. I must say that it was the first time that I regarded in a more positive light this marriage of convenience arranged by my family.

Until then, my wife had been instead an obstacle along my way toward the "bread of life", toward an eventual emergence from my clandestine faith. Day by day I had mistrusted her and her Muslim piety; I had feared that she might become uneasy about my absences and might go and denounce me.

And so I had resolved to leave her when the time came, when Massoud would come looking for me, for example. Even though I no longer really believed in that possibility, it helped me to live day by day and to tolerate that painful dissimulation of my deepest feelings.

The birth of my son, Azhar, two years previously had changed everything. Contrary to all expectations, I had become attached to that little creature, who knew nothing about his parents' history, about the hypocrisy that prevailed between the two of us. And as an indirect consequence, I also started to think well of his mother, who had given me such a gift!

From then on both of them had gained a place in my prayers, which previously had not been the case at all. Since then, in my daily petitions to God Most High, I implored him insistently to let my wife and my son become Christians someday so that they could be saved.

But in this harmonious tableau of my married life, as I pictured it to myself now, there was a discordant note: my repeated absences on Sundays; I had not really taken care to explain them to Anwar so as to avoid suspicion.

Finding the lie intolerable, I had also stopped pretending to pray in front of her. I even made so bold as to encourage her not to fast during Ramadan, telling her that I myself was not fasting.

I should have anticipated that one fine day she would ask me to give an account of my strange conduct. Probably to her way of thinking, a Musawi should be a model of piety and religious observance.

That Sunday, when I returned from Father Koder's parish, my wife planted herself in front of me, her hands on her hips, and stared at me darkly: "Are you seeing another woman?"

Usually I pretended to ignore her questions, preferring to grin and bear her eternal remonstrances [grievances]. I could have found fault with her, or scolded her, but from the outset I had decided to remain silent under her interrogations so as not to betray my secret.

Except that that day Anwar was not content with my silence: "I do not understand you. From the beginning you have been nice to me, but I feel that you are distant, dreamy, as though something were tormenting you. You do not seem to be very diligent about praying, and furthermore you lie to me!"

"What are you saying?"

"Your father and your brothers have asked me where you were, and I had thought naïvely that you were with them. Therefore I see only one explanation: you are seeing another woman!"

I was brought up short by this unusual accusation by my wife. Moreover, this quarrel in no way corresponded with my state of mind at that moment, which was rather confident and euphoric. And so, very sure of myself, I ended up spouting off to her, all at once, without any thought of the consequences: "Listen, you are wrong about the reason for my absences. I am not a sayid Musawi as you think. I am no longer Muslim; I no longer believe in Islam. I have become a Christian and I go to Mass on Sunday! That is why I am away so often. There is my secret; now you know everything."

I stopped, a little uneasy nevertheless about her reaction.

I think that I have never seen anyone lose his composure so quickly. Anwar looked as though she had been electrocuted. Her face no longer showed any sign of her fury. It gave way to such incomprehension, such confusion in confronting this situation which for her was absolutely insane, that I saw myself obliged, this time, to give her some reasons for my behavior.

So there I was, yet again forced to tell my story, from my military service through my conversion, down to my attempts to be accepted in the Church and my desire for baptism.

While speaking, I watched her reactions and trembled, finally aware that by placing myself out in the open like that I was running a great risk. If she went to denounce me to her family, I would be in a fine fix! But once I had started to confide, I could not go back. And on reflecting about it, I was not unhappy either about lancing the boil of hypocrisy in which I had been living for two years, in my own home.

Having finished my account, satisfied that my duty was done and truth was reestablished between us, I turned around to leave, wrapped in my good conscience.

To tell the truth, like a coward I preferred to bolt rather than to have to endure a scene in which I would play the villain. As for the risks that I ran on account of this conduct, I preferred not to think about them and buried them inside me.

And so I was not really surprised, when I returned, to find the house empty, my wife and child gone with their baggage. I had just enough time to wonder about their destination when a domestic servant associated with the Musawi reported to me all that had happened in my absence. Scarcely had I reached the door when Anwar picked up the telephone to call her brother to come to the rescue. She almost shouted into the handset that he should come get her and her son immediately and bring her to live with her relatives.

Instinctively I withdrew my head between my shoulders, as though to wipe off a driving rain. Indeed, it was a veritable tempest that I expected to weather in the hours to come, when I would see my in-laws arrive in force at my house to pour their contempt on my shameful conduct. Their sister had married a Christian, with all that that implies in a Shiite milieu: horror and catastrophe.

Hours passed, then days, and nothing happened. As the third day dawned, I saw the horizon clearing up and was quite happy to have weathered the storm. I still did not really know how I could emerge unscathed from that hornet's nest, but it was more promising than I had anticipated. I procrastinated another twenty-four hours and then decided to take action.

Summoning up my courage, I telephoned Anwar to ask her whether I could come see her. She seemed surprised to hear my voice, but oddly enough she said yes.

When I arrived at the house of my in-laws, I tried to put a good face on the incident, as though everything was fine, just a simple marital dispute. Deep inside I was in a tight corner.

I did not know whether they had heard the whole story, but to my great astonishment my mother-in-law and her son showed no signs of hostility. Certainly, they did not shower me with words of welcome as they usually did, but I sensed that they were more anxious about their relative than genuinely angry at me.

And then I benefited from the privileged place of the husband in Muslim society: he has every right over his wife, and so no one will ever challenge him in a marital conflict. Everyone will think that he is irreproachable.

Somewhat assured but tense, I asked to speak to Anwar alone, and the others complied. I was a little surprised to see her smile at me, and so I was the one who could hardly stammer three words.

That was not the last of the surprises: once we had isolated ourselves a bit from the rest of the family, she took the lead by declaring to me right off the bat, "I didn't tell anyone anything. When you announced that news to me, I felt that I was in a nightmare; it was as though I had been hit over the head. At first I wondered whether you had lost your mind, but I had to face the evidence: they had married me to a Christian! The first day I was so stunned that I urgently needed to tell my family. That was my initial intention, but I could do nothing about it: not one word came out of my mouth."

Anwar went on to tell me that she had eaten and drunk nothing for three days, shut up in the little room on the second floor: "My mother was worried about my lack of composure and my parched lips; she offered to call the doctor for me; she begged me to swallow a few mouthfuls of water from time to time. Nothing worked."

She had remained prostrate that entire day and part of the night, without sleeping, looking at the garden through the window and appealing to Allah.

"He alone", she continued, "could hear my complaint; I could not confide in any other human being. I asked him to enlighten me as to the truth, the true religion. I begged him to show me what I should do to get out of that pit. I was completely disoriented; I almost wanted to die."

I was dumbfounded that she had been shaken to that extent.

"And that is not all", she told me. "At the end of the third night, exhausted and at the limit of my strength, I dozed off. Then I dreamed that I was in the company of several people, around a sort of bread. They all had beautiful, smiling faces, but they were dressed in a very different way, as though they lived in another time."

I kept silent, waiting to hear the rest and inviting her to continue her story.

"There was a place for me around the table; I sat down and was about to taste the dish that they offered me, when a woman's voice interrupted me, saying, 'Wash your hands before eating!' In my dream I turned around," Anwar continued, "and I saw a very beautiful woman who was carrying a jug of water. I got up then and went over to her, and she poured water for me so that I could wash my hands and face. At that moment I woke up, with my face all wet."

Were they tears? At any rate she felt calmed, as though she had rediscovered some sort of interior peace, as though the storm had suddenly subsided. She was hungry and thirsty and asked her astonished mother to fix her a big cup of tea.

"That same day you called," she concluded her story, "and I surprised myself by smiling at you when you arrived. Now I am anxious to be with you again and for you to tell me about your secret."

I found nothing to add to that. And besides, what answer could I make? I had right before my eyes such a proof of love, whereas she could have handed me over to her family, to mine, to the whole society. It moved me all the more because, for my part, ever since our wedding I had concealed from her the truth about myself, about the things that I considered fundamental.

I still did not expect that the crisis would be resolved that easily. Yet with the same simplicity I suggested that she return to our house, with our son. She agreed without a moment's hesitation, with a nod of her head, as though nothing had happened.

Actually that was not entirely true. Something had changed—between us. What had changed was her, and me, and that little seed of confidence sowed between the two of us, this secret that belonged only to us and which bound us together from then on much more than when we were married officially.

Betting on this brand-new confidence, I opened my heart to her that same evening and told her the unvarnished truth, unreservedly. I told her about myself, about my faith, and about my love for this Jesus. I so wanted to see her share this enthusiasm that motivated me so profoundly. But I did not want to force her: "Nothing obliges you to follow me in my faith; I want you to feel completely free. But if you wish, I will help you; I will show you the way that I have already traveled."

Indeed, I had in mind the method of Massoud, which did not work so badly with me; could it perhaps succeed with Anwar, too?

I sensed that she was undecided, unsettled by my proposal, divided between her Muslim faith and the attraction to Christ that I was telling her about. Would she dare to take another step and call her own religion into question for love's sake?

Given her hesitation, I suggested a line of reasoning: "What you can do is to reread the Qur'an, or we can read it together, if you like, while trying to understand it. Only then will you decide which religion seems better to you. But you are not obliged to give me an answer now."

Maybe she should sleep on it; that might enable her to overcome her misgivings, I told myself, while praying silently that she would make the right choice.

The following morning, Anwar announced to me that she was willing to take the gamble, even though it frightened her a little. She also agreed that I should serve as her guide in this adventure, the outcome of which no one could foretell. My wife certainly had courage!

From then on I worked zealously to bring to her attention the verses from the Qur'an that had seemed to me the thorniest, for example, the ones that talk about the way in which women are considered. My object was to save her time in her reflections while avoiding my own comments on those passages.

I wanted her to do the work herself, in the private arena of her conscience. That is how Massoud had left me free to choose. That is how I wanted to proceed with my wife.

I also encouraged her to read the Gospel [Bible], which I quoted to her at every turn, since it seemed to me that I knew it by heart. I felt that the flame of my love for Christ touched her.

"My heart burns when I listen to you talk about Jesus", she told me one day. "When I hear you I even wonder whether you might not have actually met him. But when I hear the way in which you speak about the Qur'an and criticize it, it frightens me."

That was the hardest thing for her: to detach herself from what Islam had always taught her, especially what it says about Christians. So much so, that it took a week for her to dare just to take the Gospel in her hands; she did this with fear and trembling, even though I made sure to close the door of our room before bringing the Bible out from under my shirt, where it was held safely by my belt.

From that moment on she had a lasting passion for that account. She spent hours reading the life of Jesus, and she fell in love with this book that spoke to her about love and hope.

The result was that in six months at most Anwar came to abandon the Qur'an. She could no longer believe a book that, she declared, treated women so harshly.

I was overjoyed when she even asked to go with me to Mass occasionally on Sunday, with our son, Azhar, since she was curious to learn about the community of the disciples of Jesus! She told me that she was surprised to see how the women are viewed differently than in Islam and how they are respected.

When we traveled by car to Mass, her greatest pleasure was to take off her veil and throw it out the window, which obliged us to buy one each time on the return trip! But money was not a problem for me, and I was happy to see her so relieved by removing that iron collar from her head. The gesture was very important for her: it signified her rejection of the considerable burden that Muslim society caused to weigh on her.

For me, it was also a fine present that she gave me, enabling us in this way to reunite our little family around the person of Christ. But I knew also, because I remained lucid and she had told me, that she would not go any further in questioning her life.

For if she were to follow this discrediting of Islam to its logical conclusion, she knew very well that she would have to burn the bridges to her own family, for whom religion and social life were one and the same reality. And for her that was out of the question! No longer to see her seven brothers and sisters, who were all very close, to break off relations with her mother—that was unimaginable for Anwar, who called her mother two or three times a day to ask her how a dish should be salted [seasoned].

At the beginning of my conversion, I naïvely thought that I would be able to use my influence on my family, particularly on my father, to exhort them to change their religion. At that time it was all Massoud could do to dissuade me from even trying.

From that perspective, Anwar was much more realistic than I about the possibility of changing the order of things in that Iraqi Muslim society. She knew intuitively that her mother and her brothers and sisters would never question their own religion.

In a certain way, Islam also meant security for her, the security provided by the proximity of her family and the security of a well-established life. For my wife, renouncing Islam officially and openly would mean leaving everything that was reassuring for an unknown life whose contours she could not yet discern but which never stopped worrying her.

After several months, Anwar took another step. She told me that she wanted to come with me to meet Father Koder, to have him speak to us about the truths of the faith. These regular evenings, which very quickly became a weekly event, increased our thirst to hear about the things of God.

Little by little the priest set us free of our Islamic culture, which very often falsified our understanding of Scripture. For instance, in the passage where Jesus warns against giving the bread of the children of God to the "dogs", still being Muslims despite ourselves, we saw that as an insult, a reminder of the term "infidels", rather than as an incentive to go further in the faith, to be converted more and more.

Father Koder also taught us the wisdom of the Fathers of the Church, with a calm authority that left both of us amazed and silent during the whole trip back.

One evening Anwar broke that meditative silence, which had become a habit, to announce to me in her sweet voice, "Muhammad, I have chosen Christ."

I was not sure that I had heard her correctly. Was she truly announcing this news to me, something so prodigious that I had ceased to expect it ages ago?

During those two years I had grown used to the idea that she was becoming wedded to the religious status quo, by which she was torn, I knew, but incapable of deciding one way or the other.

And so as not to make the situation even more painful for her, I no longer dared to ask her about her faith. It may have been a bit selfish on my part, but for me it was enough that Anwar went with me to Mass, that we loved its religious atmosphere, and that she took part in our meetings with Father Koder. I did not feel that I had the right to be constantly calibrating the extent of her attachment to Christianity.

Those few words, pronounced in a low voice, on a hot summer night, were to upset the equilibrium of our life, and even our bank balance. Most importantly, they revealed to me a facet of my wife's personality that I knew absolutely nothing about. I was flabbergasted. I realized that right before my eyes she had just accomplished something that I thought myself incapable of: [taking] such a daring act of faith that it was like a great leap into the void.

I had had the benefit of that dream, of my vision, to bring me to the turning point of my whole life. That was not the case with Anwar. And yet she made that decision that testified to an extraordinary degree of courage. I almost had the impression that before that moment I had not really known my wife.

To all appearances, however, there was no real change in our daily life, in the daytime at least. In the evening we continued our comings and goings while concealing our intentions and motivating force from our respective families. Although our household was strengthened by it, the distance from our close relatives increased: they did not seem to notice the slightest change in us. And we did nothing to undeceive them.

Between Anwar and me, this upheaval, by a process of mutual reinforcement, increased our yearning for a complete Christian life: we wanted to be baptized. And that was one thing that the priest who was instructing us did not seem ready to grant us, no doubt for fear of confronting his hierarchy.

As for me, I was constantly torn by the desire to receive Communion. Far from being extinguished as time went on, this desire became stronger with each failure that I experienced. The longing to eat that bread of life was so keen that I was ready to do anything to satisfy it, even to steal the Eucharist if necessary. One time at Mass I got in line to receive Communion with my head down, hoping that the priest would not recognize me. At the last moment, I stepped out of the line, unable to look the priest in the face.

Spurred on by the new determination of my wife and by my own hunger, I once again began to look for other churches in Baghdad that might respond favorably to our request for baptism.

After four or five months of fruitless investigations in the old districts of the city populated by Christians, I happened one day upon a friary, in a more modern quarter. Somewhat intimidated, I rang at the door of that modern building, which was of modest size and topped with a bell tower without a cross. A friar answered abruptly, with a strong foreign accent, "What do you want?"

Once again I presented my case in a few words, once again requesting baptism. Again a refusal: "It is not possible! Look elsewhere."

But this time I did not let myself be put off; I had had enough of being turned away.

"I will not leave here until I have a clear explanation of the reasons for this refusal."

"Listen, I really don't have the time now, I have a lot of things to do. But you can talk to another friar who has been here a long time. Maybe he can give you an answer. Moreover, he speaks Arabic."

That was not really a promise; it was not even much of a lead. But it was better than nothing. I decided to be content with a telephone number for today.

That same evening I contacted the religious that he had referred me to, Father Gabriel. Having learned from experience, I strove to be explicit enough about my faith experience while still remaining vague, and so I managed without too much difficulty to get an appointment for the following week.

Six days later, a very tall, middle-aged man invited me into his cell. What struck me most was his luminous expression. His blue eyes reflected great kindness, and when he looked at me I felt that at that moment I was the most important man in the world for that friar.

He had the appearance of a Westerner—he told me that he was originally from Switzerland—but he expressed himself quite eloquently in Arabic, better than I could.

"I learned the grammar," he explained to me with a smile, "and I have been here in Iraq for forty years now."

From the outset the man inspired confidence, and I got the impression that I was not the only person in this situation. Behind him, beneath the crucifix, there were several photos, showing him surrounded by children, by smiling families with joyful faces, one with nuns. "Those women are four sisters from a Palestinian family who lived right beside the convent", he told me in a confidential tone. "In the other photos you can see some Muslim families who have invited me to break the fast during Ramadan."

He seemed in no hurry to get to the heart of the matter and asked me no questions. He acted as though he did not notice my impatience.

I could not stand it any longer. I took advantage of a pause in his reminiscences to launch into a plea for my cause. He listened to me with his head leaning forward, his eyes half-closed. Only a few approving nods assured me that he was listening attentively. Otherwise I might have thought that he had fallen asleep.

When I stopped speaking there was a long silence while he reflected, disturbed only by the regular ticktock of a mechanical alarm clock. I held my breath for fear of breaking his intense concentration. I anxiously watched the rhythm of his eyebrows, which knitted and relaxed with his train of thought—as though he was weighing the pros and cons, discerning his duty between the risks and the state of necessity in which I found myself.

Suddenly he raised his head again. He looked at me intensely, fixedly, detaching his words slightly so as to engrave them in my mind: "I agree to baptize you, but first you have to be instructed in the articles of faith."

No doubt it was the solemnity of the tone of voice used by that friar, or else I had become circumspect because of the disappointments and setbacks and inured by the time and perseverance that it had taken, or maybe it was quite simply the seriousness of the moment. I received that statement, a favorable one, nevertheless, with a restraint that I had not thought myself capable of.

On second thought, perhaps I also intuited that the preparation for baptism by Father Gabriel would not be done hastily. He scheduled for us, with our consent, of course, an intensive series of sessions; I met with him several times a week, either alone or with Anwar. There were even weeks when we spent four evenings with him, for weighty discussions that lasted long hours, sometimes four or five at a stretch.

During these sessions we developed bonds of friendship with him that we did not have with Father Koder. I must say that the man who for us quickly became Abouna Gabriel, that is, Our Father Gabriel, was a marvelous instructor in the faith: he could be gentle and tactful in transmitting his love of God.

But he was also very aware of his charism and of the influence that he had on those around him. He wisely and scrupulously made sure that the faith that he taught was clearly distinguished from any attachment to him personally, to the point of seeming gruff, cold, and offensive when he felt that there was some danger of confusion. Once we were rebuked sharply for having complimented him on the way in which he explained the sacrament of baptism to us: "Don't thank me! I had nothing to do with it. I am just an instrument in the hands of the Holy Spirit, nothing more!"

I could not argue with him about that. We were so attached to Abouna Gabriel that we changed our parish on Sunday so as to come to the church adjoining the friary. It was large and could hold as many as two hundred people. We went there as a family, with Azhar, whom we taught to make the sign of the cross on entering the church.

Fatwa

Baghdad, June 1997

As the years went by, the great caution that I had adopted in dealing with my family was dulled. Although I still was very careful to disguise from them my activities in the evenings and on Sundays, I stopped pretending to adhere to Islam, first of all, because in the long run that hypocrisy had become intolerable to me, and also because of the unremitting schedule of meetings with Abouna Gabriel in recent months.

For example, it had become almost impossible for me to continue to accompany the whole tribe to Karbala every Thursday. Located around one hundred kilometers [62 miles] to the southwest of Baghdad, this Shiite place of pilgrimage stood at the very spot where they decapitated the imam Hussein ben Ali, the grandson of Muhammad.

At first I gave as my excuse [that I had] an urgent meeting or a headache, or that my wife was ill, but then later, nothing. For very quickly these deceptive excuses no longer convinced anyone. And so each time they asked me another question, I answered quite simply that I did not feel like going, that it no longer interested me.

There was just one little detail: I was still the heir apparent, and my absence was noticed more than any other in the populous tribe of the Musawi, especially because previously I had often been the one who had the honor of driving the family bus.

Several times, especially at the beginning of my search in Baghdad, I felt like confiding in my father. I still had affection for him, and it grieved me to betray his trust in that way. But how could I convince him that I had chosen the right path, when I myself was being driven away from the churches as though I were unclean? There was an inconsistency in it that I could never have managed to explain with solid arguments. Therefore I regretfully never acted on my initial intention.

One fine summer evening, while returning [home] with Anwar from a session with Abouna Gabriel, we noticed an unusual agitation at the house, especially at that late hour. Something like a slight feeling of panic prevailed.

When she heard us arrive, the maid dashed to meet us, quite scared. At our urgent questions she burst into tears and answered that in our absence my brothers had come to search the house.

I began to understand and was worried about our children: our son, Azhar, and our daughter, Miamy, who was scarcely one month old. I called her [my daughter] that out of defiance, because my family had forced on her a traditional Arabic name that I did not want, Maimouneh.

"The little girl is still sleeping, but Azhar was awakened by the ruckus", the maid told me. "When he saw that it was his uncles, he began to give them big smiles."

"And then what happened?!" I shouted, sensing that there must be some other reason for her tears.

"Then they found a book that they called a blasphemous book."

So they had laid hands on my Bible. I had hidden it carefully, however, behind other much more presentable books.

"Is there anything else that you want to tell me?"

"Yes."

"Speak!"

"They went back to Azhar and smiled with him and asked him what he did every Sunday with his parents."

"And then?"

The words shattered inside of me:

"It was awful", she replied with a long sob. "He answered by making over himself the sign of the Christians, the sign of the cross!"

I looked at my wife without saying anything. I was incapable of reacting to that news, which was fraught with dangers for the future. Anwar kept her cool and sent the maid away, so that we could consider what course of action to take.

I sprawled on the cushions in the living room and nervously lit a cigarette. All sorts of questions jostled in my head, but I could not manage to pin one down. What should we do? Flee? But with no idea where to go, that would be condemning ourselves to wander endlessly. Confront my father immediately for an explanation? That would be acknowledging that I was in the wrong.

After all, I should have expected that one day this lie that I had been living for so many years would suddenly come to light. I would have been almost relieved, if I had not been so worried about my wife and my son. I would have to play a careful game with my father, I calculated, so as to maintain a more or less normal life for them.

For a long time that night, lying on my bed, I turned the situation over and over in every direction, but without arriving at a satisfactory solution. I ended up dozing off into a troubled sleep.

The next morning at dawn I was awakened by repeated knocks drumming on the front door. I emerged with difficulty from my torpor, only to hear one of my brothers tell me that my father wanted to see me immediately about an important matter.

I dressed hastily, still drowsy after so little sleep. I hardly had the strength to wonder about the reason for the "all hands on deck" so early in the morning. It was quite unusual, but I did not immediately make the connection with what had happened the day before.

While I was walking up the road that led to my father's imposing mansion, the thought occurred to me: what if my father himself was calling for the explanation that had been put off so many times? But if so, why so early?

I had little time to reflect further. I turned the doorknob at the entrance: no one there! The brother who was accompanying me then broke the silence of our short walk; my father was waiting for me in the grand reception room. That was standing on ceremony. Why did it have to happen in such an official place?

The answer was not long in coming. I scarcely had time to cross the threshold [when] in a fraction of a second, a multitude of arms were beating down on me—like a violent hailstorm.

Instinctively I raised my hands to protect myself. I no longer saw anything; I could not distinguish faces. I felt the blows raining down and my inability to respond. Very quickly someone bound my hands behind my back with handcuffs. My feet were surrounded with chains. A strong voice ordered me to get down: "On your knees!"

I was petrified—fear in the gut, knees trembling. Yet I had the strength to raise my head to see who my aggressors were.

To my great surprise, my own brothers were there with my uncles and my cousins; among them was Hassan, the one who was a member of the secret service. I had never seen such a thing! They were pointing pistols and submachine guns at me. I was looking at a nightmare vision that seemed to be unreal, but also terribly threatening.

My mind was racing and panicked, refusing to understand. Suddenly I noticed my father, who had stayed back somewhat. I stared at him imploringly and asked, "Father, what is happening to me? Why?" But the words stuck in my constricted throat. In return I had only his dark eyes, which he darted at me like lightning bolts.

All at once his fury exploded uncontrollably: "What is happening to you? You are becoming a Christian? You are totally sick! Do you realize the shame that that will bring upon me, your father? When young people just become Sunnis, even their relatives are no longer allowed to visit us

Shiites or to come to our mosques. And you think of being a Christian son! That leaves me no alternative but to put on a veil in order to go out into the street, like your mother."

His diatribe struck me deep in the heart. I nearly lost my temper and felt like shouting at him and telling him that I couldn't care less about his reputation or what Shiite society would think. If that was the most important thing for him, then we had nothing else to say to each other.

But I kept quiet—because I was in a humiliating position of weakness. I also sensed strongly that all of this was irrational, that everything could tip over in a second, in that tense, electrically charged atmosphere.

I no longer recognized my relatives. Those who were carrying weapons, I could tell, were ready to lean on the trigger at the slightest gesture, at the slightest word of contradiction. Something like a wind of madness was blowing on everyone around me.

Even my mother, my own mother, who had just made her appearance in the room, was uttering words of unprecedented violence: "Kill him and throw him in the Basel!"

What reply could I make to that? If I were thrown into that subterranean canal which empties into salt water, my body would disappear completely, like everything that falls into the Basel. My mother was thus making it very clear that she wanted to wipe out every trace of my existence, to cut me out of her memory.

I was totally helpless. There was nothing for me to do except resign myself to die. I lowered my head again, ready to hear that sentence that would end my life.

Interminable minutes passed. Nothing happened. I was sweating fear through all the pores of my skin. Suddenly, without warning, they all left the room, one after the other, without saying another word, as though they had realized that they had gone too far, or else a strong authority—my father's?—had brought them to their senses.

Then I was alone in the large room. I strained my ears to hear their discussions outside. They were all talking at the same time, and I could make out only snatches, phrases spoken by those who raised their voices above the uproar and confusion. "What are we going to do with him? . . . afraid of scandal . . . get rid of him secretly . . . Najaf."

All my senses were on the alert; I tried to put the puzzle together but saw nothing good in what I had heard. I did not understand what the mausoleum of Najaf had to do with this story. It is the third most important shrine of Shiite Islam, located two hundred kilometers [124 miles] away; it is also the center of Shiite political power in this country. Did that mean that I was going to be brought before the highest authorities? I did not think that my case was so serious.

I was still wondering, when hands laid hold of me so as to carry me to the trunk of a car. The driver floored the accelerator and the tires squealed. The shock absorbers were worn out, and I was tossed around to the rhythm of the potholes along the dirt road. Since my hands were still bound behind my back, I had no way of cushioning the shocks.

Soon the car stabilized and began to run more regularly. We must have taken the highway. This seemed to confirm the hypothesis about Najaf.

But, why? I was reduced to endless speculations in the darkness of the trunk. They all led to an almost certain result: death. I did not see how I could get out of this trap set by my own relatives. Of course I had expected that someday a conflict would erupt with my family, but I had not reckoned how much shame the conversion of one of their own would mean to them—and it did not matter which one!

This was the only plausible explanation for the hatred that had poured down on me that morning: fear of public scandal. If my change of religion were to become known, my family could lose everything: its honor, its importance, and its status in Shiite society.

Nor did I forget that eliminating apostates is a rule that has been enforced since the appearance of Islam and is repeated in the hadiths [written traditions about the Prophet, Muhammad]—sometimes, as in my case, to the detriment of the love that unites the members of the same family.

Finally, I ended up concluding fatalistically that those same social and religious pressures may have allowed me to stay alive for a few more hours: eliminating me too close to the family home involved a certain risk of being seen—and thus of raising questions.

[This was a] small consolation, really, if it had to end in the same way. The only thing that mattered to me now was the prospect of dying without having been baptized, and a question, or rather an inconsistency in the divine plan that I could not manage to account for: why I had experienced all this for nothing, or almost.

The car stopped brutally. As I listened to the doors slam, I expected the worst and started praying as though my last hour had arrived. But nothing happened.

I waited for several minutes, with my breathing almost stopped and my ears on the alert for the slightest sound that might give me some clue about the course of events. Still, nothing.

Anxiety gripped me by the throat. To overcome it, I started to move my arms gently, because they were stiff from being in that extremely uncomfortable position. About an hour passed, which seemed interminable.

Suddenly I heard footsteps approaching. Immediately I was aroused from my torpor, nerves taut. The same hands, those of my brothers, unceremoniously lifted me out of the trunk and pushed me to my feet. I then recognized the two golden minarets flanking the tomb of [Imam] Ali [Bnu Abi Talib]. So we were in Najaf.

But I had no time to gush about the beauty of the shrine; I was led roughly to a building located on one side. There a surprise was waiting for me inside, big-time: there I was, in the presence of the highest Shiite authority in Iraq, the ayatollah Muhammad Sadr[4]—a very prominent personage, who justified a trip like that.

He was a very upright man, and very direct, too. I had met him long ago when he was preaching vigorously one Friday evening at the mosque, sword in hand, to add a bold gesture to his audacious words. Today, I was afraid instead that he would thrust his sword through my back, on the spot. For if my father had had recourse to that very influential man, who was consulted in delicate situations, it was certainly not just to get two or three unimportant pieces of advice.

Therefore my case was serious, even terribly worrisome, as difficult as it could be, since it required the intervention of the greatest ayatollah of the country. I was in a tight spot, trembling about the outcome, getting ready to appear before a special tribunal before being executed.

Affably, however, and full of forbearance, the ayatollah began by asking someone to remove my chains. No one budged. He did not insist. Then for about ten minutes he sang the praises of Islam and its grandeur while at the same time disparaging Christianity as much as he could, which was contemptible in his eyes.

[4] The father of Moktada Sadr. He was later killed by Saddam Hussein.

At the end of his oration, which had not moved me in the least, I asked to speak, with an assurance that surprised even me: "I have listened to you attentively. What proof do you have that I am a Christian?"

"What about the books?"

"I have other books in my library—some poetry, books about geography and medicine. That does not make me a poet or a physician! It interests me; I feel like learning, that is all."

"And your son, who makes the sign of the cross?"

I looked at my brothers, who were standing around me. Their faces were hard, unfeeling. I got the impression that this was payback for the influence that I had over them for all those years. Their hatred for me did not completely surprise me; my disappearance would restart speculations about who would be the next chief of the Musawi. It would also protect them from any possible vengeance on my part.

Even though I was chained, I despised their incidental superiority, the kind that cowards have: "That is not a valid argument", I replied, suddenly inspired. "My brothers have been jealous of me for a long time. They may have invented the story to take the money from my inheritance."

I sensed that I had sown doubt in the mind of my interlocutor. From then on he was no longer that sure of being in the right. The ayatollah then took my father by the hand and led him apart from the group for a new deliberation.

Cold sweats again. The tension in the room was palpable. For about twenty minutes not a word was exchanged between me and my brothers and cousins. We all were awaiting the verdict.

It was pronounced by Muhammad Sadr: "If it is confirmed that he is a Christian, then he must be killed, and Allah will reward the one who carries out this fatwa."

All at once I could breathe more easily, as though they had taken a weight off my shoulders. Those words meant that I had a reprieve, a delay in the execution of that death sentence.

They immediately took me back to the car, without any further discussion. Once again I was shoved into the trunk. I supposed that we would make the return trip to Baghdad.

In my rolling sarcophagus, I went over in an endless loop the surprising dialogue that had just unfolded. I was astonished in particular by the responses that had occurred to me: they had been appropriate, full of a pertinence that was not like me. Most of all, they had caused the ayatollah himself to relent. This was strange, since usually I am rather slow and not really a good speaker.

For me there was no doubt at all: I had been inspired by the Holy Spirit. It was due to him that I was still alive at that hour—and maybe also thanks to my father. For he was the one who had channeled the fury of my brothers and cousins that morning by having them leave the room and probably directing them toward the arbitration of Muhammad Sadr.

My father, Fadel-Ali, was also the one who had discussed with the ayatollah what sanction to adopt in my case, preferring a serious warning to an immediate execution. I deduced from this that my father had not really wanted me to be put to death. He wanted to intimidate me, so that I would return to a better attitude toward Islam, to a more convenient way of thinking about religion.

Despite all appearances, I found it very difficult to imagine that every trace of his attachment to me had abruptly disappeared. But I was still not in the clear either, and I had no idea what sort of fate I had in store.

The Trial

Al-Hakimieh, Baghdad, June 1997

Two hours later, when the trunk was opened again, it was night. I found myself alone, so to speak, with my cousin from the secret service, in an immense parking lot. The rest of my family had disappeared.

In front of me was a large, white, three-story building, the length of which increased with each level, which made it look like a ship. I recognized it as the most terrifying prison in Baghdad, which was sadly infamous. Saddam Hussein incarcerated all his opponents there—politicians, Kurds, Shiites, prisoners of war, as well as major criminals—until they were judged and then sent to the other big prison, Abu Ghraib. Before the embargo, it was the prison for foreigners. Today it had become also the headquarters for the tribunal of the secret service police, Jihaz al-Mukhabarat al-Amma [Iraqi Intelligence Service], a place of tortures and summary executions.

I understood better why my cousin Hassan, a member of that secret police, was the only one to have remained that evening. His was not the friendliest presence, since it was as cold as though we were strangers and consisted of bringing me within the walls of the building to hand me over to some uniformed men. They must have been members of the secret service also, because they exchanged among themselves signs of collusion from which I was excluded.

For them I became the prisoner, someone who would be added to the thousands of others detained in that sinister prison. From now on I was on my own; my cousin left without saying a word to me. Despite the mildness of the weather, I shivered as I uneasily examined my guardians. My fate hung on their every word. I felt weak, helpless, abandoned by everyone.

The humiliation, however, was only beginning. First they asked me rudely to take off all my clothes, without exception. At no time did they offer me an isolated place so that I could avoid exposing my nudity to strangers. I swallowed my shame at the indifferent looks of the armed men; then they gave me a patched, threadbare outfit.

After having me sit down at a table, they pointed to a form to be filled out with the names of my father and my mother, as well as my address. Only then did they speak directly to me, in a dry tone of voice: "Now you will forget your name: you will answer when they call the number 318."

"What if I don't remember it?"

We must have exceeded the time permitted for speaking to prisoners. Without further explanation, one of the guardians wrote the number on my forearm and blindfolded me. Flanked by two giants with powerful hands, I was led through a maze of corridors. We took a grating elevator—another maze. And finally we arrived in a room where they gestured for me to remove my blindfold.

I found myself in a very small cell, scarcely two meters by two meters [43 square feet], with bright red wallpaper, a little window, and a lamp embedded in the wall behind a grille. The iron door that closed behind me was heavy and thick. It snapped shut with a dry clack that startled me. In the middle of the door was a narrow opening to pass a bowl through.

I collapsed onto the ground, exhausted by the day's emotions. And I fell asleep almost immediately on the hard floor: a heavy, agitated sleep.

The next morning I was awakened at dawn by the daylight. I had the impression of being groggy, as though I had drunk throughout the previous evening: my brain was hazy and my forehead ached. A long wait then began, which was scarcely disturbed when a plate of soup was offered me disdainfully through the little slot in the door.

In that tiny room, the scarlet décor did not foster optimism. On the contrary, it oppressed me, hemmed me in, and made me anxious. The summer sun caused brilliant, almost dazzling, reflections here and there. As the hours were slowly consumed, one by one, my imagination got carried away. It was my own blood spread out before my eyes on the wall. With horror I sensed that I could read in it my future.

Most of the time, the waiting was painful. I wanted to be delivered from the unknown fate that awaited me, lurking in the darkness and threatening. But even my pain became dull and led to apathy. I lost all sense of time. Only the little window through which I saw a bit of sky still connected me to the succession of days and nights.

On the third day I heard the lock click three times. The heavy door opened, pulled by two guards. I looked at them inquisitively to discern their intentions and to prepare myself for the unavoidable. But their expressions were frustratingly bland. I was reduced to following them passively, head down, like a lamb being led to the slaughterhouse.

Speaking of livestock, it was more like a cattle car. In bewilderment I entered another cell; it was bright red also and the same size as the earlier one, but in it there were already sixteen other detainees!

My guardians asked me whether I recognized anyone in that room and, reassured by my negative reply, unceremoniously pushed me in and closed the door.

In the silence that had fallen at my arrival, I stared each of the prisoners in the face. These were the men with whom I was going to share the few square centimeters that I had a right to. I received a vague smile of welcome here, a hostile glare tinged with curiosity there; most of the faces were resigned and scarcely paid me any attention.

I tried somehow or other to find a place for myself without disturbing the other occupants when one of them asked me my name. I then proudly stood up straight and declared in a loud voice, "I am a Musawi, from Baghdad!"

The aristocratic Shiite family name rang like a pistol shot in the little overpopulated room. Now all eyes were turned toward me, staring at me with interest. I noted with some satisfaction that even in this repulsive place, the power of my tribe still earned me respect and attention. It was perhaps my last remaining dignity, but in those circumstances I hung on to it like a life preserver so as not to sink into despair.

"Number 318!" The voice from outside barked the order imperiously. It immediately brought down what was left of my pride. Sighing, I returned to my humiliating status and edged toward the door as my fellow detainees watched and pitied me. I was hardly reassured by their commiseration.

Flanked by two convict-gang guards, I walked down the stairs to the basement. Every time we made contact, the jailers took the opportunity to jab me several times with their elbows in the sides or in the stomach. I put up with it, stifling cries of pain.

Downstairs my fears increased even more when they blindfolded me. They bound my hands behind my back. "This is it", I thought; "my hour has come." So I was going to end my life in the underworld of that infamous prison.

But the men surrounding me seemed to have other intentions. I heard someone rummaging in a closet, and then they brought a videocassette and some files up to my bound hands so that I could touch them.

"Here is the evidence", a dry voice in front of me explained, "of your guilt. But if you tell us everything that you know, maybe we can be lenient."

"What have I done?" I asked them without hesitation.

"We know that you have attended some churches belonging to the Christians. Which churches? Who are those Christians? Where do they live? Who is the first Christian who dared to speak to you? That is what we want to know. If you tell us, you will become for us just a simple witness and no longer a criminal. Speak!"

I answered nothing, thinking at top speed, goaded by fear. On the one hand I could perhaps save my skin, but on the other hand, if I gave them names, I would be putting the whole Christian community in Iraq in danger. At that moment I suddenly remembered something that Abouna Gabriel said: "In asking for baptism, you are [not only] risking your own life, but also the lives of the Christians who will have responded to your request." And I had no desire to sacrifice those who had become dear to me through our common faith.

Following an inspiration, I finally retorted to the men who were subjecting me to that interrogation, "I know neither Christian nor church."

The answer must not have pleased the two men stationed behind my back. Blows rained down. Fists, slaps, kicks—I collapsed beneath the violence, which assaulted every last bit of my body. With my hands still bound, I had no way to protect myself.

I curled up on the floor, short of breath. All my flesh was screaming for mercy, but I did not unclench my teeth. In a flash of lucidity I tried to turn my face toward the ground to protect it from the heavy shoes of the guards.

The ordeal lasted a good ten minutes; then my torturers stopped, swearing and panting. I clung to that moment of respite, waiting for their reactions. In a few minutes I had become timid, like a beaten dog that watches his master's riding-whip and begs for pity with his eyes.

"Give us names! Who are the Christians that you met?"

"I do not know any Christians."

One of the two torturers left the room. Five more minutes passed. I tried to catch my breath and to examine my wounds mentally. In the brutality of that avalanche of blows, my blindfold had shifted. I could see with one eye what was going on around me.

With terror I saw the second guard reappear. In his hands he had a long piece of electrical cable, at least two or three centimeters [approximately 1 inch] thick. The man sneered as he looked at me, with a horrible expression. He seemed crazed with a murderous, bestial madness, as though inebriated by the cruelty of his act.

All my muscles tensed, waiting to receive the first shock. The pain was atrocious, inhumane. It wrested from me a cry that came from the depths of my gut; the echo of it reverberated endlessly in the maze of rooms and somber corridors. But I knew that I had no hope of any help in that dismal place. So I kept quiet.

This had the effect of increasing the ill humor of my assailant: my silence was to him like a red flag. He vented his fury on me, using even more force.

The same muscular interrogation occurred every day, or nearly so, for almost three months. I rarely spent three days without going into the depths of the prison to undergo my Calvary.

As I descended several flights on foot, I begged the Holy Spirit to give me fortitude, knowing full well that I would have to climb those same steps again on all fours.

Oddly, after four or five strokes of the whip, the pain lessened, until it completely disappeared, as though my brain, saturated with suffering, refused to recognize any more. Or was I growing accustomed to it?

It helped me, in any case, to keep my misfortune at a distance. One day I even managed to find the courage to question my tormentor, who was out of breath from striking me: "Why do you hit me like that? Do you know me?"

"I am just doing my job", he replied, without an ounce of remorse.

A terrifying answer, from which I also drew the courage to hold my tongue, so as not to give my torturers what they wanted or to betray the Christians of Baghdad who had helped me.

My job was to keep silence. What enabled me to endure was the awareness that I had been spared miraculously and was still alive after having suffered the worst possible disgrace. Morally and socially, I had already fallen from a great height: the treachery of my family, the fatwa of the ayatollah. I had held on by virtue of an unknown strength that I had not suspected. I was not about to flinch now when faced with physical torture.

And so my mind remained steadfast. It lessened, as though by magic, the force of the blows that I received. But my body retained the memory of it over the course of the following days. Those were the most difficult moments, when the shooting pain became sharp and unbearable. I could scarcely stand up in that little cell, stiff and bent over like an old man before my time.

My only help came from the memory of the lives of the martyrs that I had read after my conversion. I did not recall each one of the stories precisely, but they had left me with one conviction, just one, which was more precious than a diamond in those accursed days: "No one ever becomes a Christian on a bed of roses."

I clung to that idea that there is a price to pay, and in my case that price was not cheap. In my prayers, certain phrases from the Gospels occurred to me over and over. They were among the few that still managed to catch my exhausted attention: "You will be hated by all for my name's sake"

(Lk 21:17), or else, "I have not come to bring peace, but a sword" (Mt 10:34).

Paradoxically, these terrible statements helped me to hold on; they gave me comfort. For me they were the sign that I was not on the wrong track. Deep down, I was not far from desiring that martyrdom which would prove definitively my zeal for Christ.

Yet at the same time I regularly experienced anger when I looked at the injustice of the trial that I was enduring, an anger that sometimes went so far as to be murderous. The desire to kill my torturers then rose within me like a fire and completely overwhelmed me. To exculpate myself for thinking this, I imagined that in acting that way I would at least have the satisfaction of vindicating the violence with which I was being treated.

The interrogations stopped suddenly, without any reason. I still trembled, day after day, at every noise on the other side of the door. After a week, I allowed myself once more to hope that I had survived that terrible adversity— certainly, at the price of enormous sufferings, but it also filled me with such a sense of gratitude! That mitigated the pain of my black bruises.

I had not reached the end of my afflictions, however. I would now be confronted with another kind of suffering, more cruel because it was psychological. It was probably even more severe than the physical ordeal: I was left to myself, locked up the whole day, and for an indefinite time, in that cell from which I was never let out. Henceforth my enemies were named isolation, hunger, and squalor, which were worsened by the absence of any prospect of a change in my condition.

Three months before, when I had been arrested, I had not even had the time to have breakfast. Since then, I had been hungry. At every moment that atrocious feeling tormented me; it directed every one of my thoughts. Now I reflected only to the rhythm of my stomach and of the food that the prison guards brought me.

Even the word "food" seemed rather inappropriate to describe the tepid white water that they served us in the morning, which was supposed to be soup. Instead of soup it must have been the water used to cook rice, but without any rice in it. Since the prison was overpopulated, the cooks who were expected to feed everybody had probably chosen that dish because it was considerably more economical.

At midday the soup was yellow in color. It must have contained some chicken. And in the evening, the red liquid suggested tomatoes. In short, although we did not have the contents, at least the colors gave us the illusion of variety in the menu.

Since all of us in the cell were famished, we had developed an extremely rigorous system of sharing the meager food that they brought us as well as possible, without causing tension.

When it was a hunk of bread, for example, we even kept track of the crumbs. And when, oh happy day, we had the right to a few pieces of chicken or meat, nothing remained after it was divided up minutely, not even the bones. Sometimes just a bit of bone was saved from the spoils and was used to mend our uniforms, which were worn and threadbare.

To drink, we had to cool the water from the shower, which was intentionally made boiling hot during meals— the supreme torture devised for those who had committed the worst crimes against the security of the Iraqi state.

I really had no animosity toward my fellow detainees. But I felt no particular affinity with them. In my case the privations and the persecution compounded my distress at not being able to speak about the accusations against me. The others did not abstain from recounting their misdeeds loud and long; indeed, they boasted of their crimes. Then I would keep quiet, striving to remain aloof and not participating much in the discussions, although they involved me in them.

Besides, I was in a political prison, where they incarcerated government officials and military officers, some of whom were condemned to death. Therefore it was very likely that the conversations of these criminals against the state were under surveillance, especially when the discussion revolved around the political regime.

And when we addressed religious questions, I felt even less impelled to give my opinion. What could I say to my cellmates, both Shiites and Sunnis, who endlessly debated who the legitimate successor of the prophet Muhammad was, Abou Bakr for the Sunnis, or Ali for the Shiites?

Therefore I kept silence, for fear of uttering excessively harsh words about the Prophet himself.

Besides, I had already tempted fate by declaring loud and long that I could not pray in such a dirty place and that at any rate a Musawi went directly to heaven. That allowed me to remain aloof during prayer, without incurring the thunderbolts of the Wahhabis, the most radical Sunni movement that there is. In other circumstances such words could certainly have meant death for me. Here in prison, the power of those sectarians was limited, and the name of Musawi made them respect me. So they left me alone.

The isolation weighed heavily on me, but it also had a positive result: it enabled me to deepen my faith.

Until now I had been experiencing combat, with my one desire being to have myself baptized. All my energy had been concentrated on that goal; anything that ran contrary to it I considered an obstacle to be removed—whereas here, in this little cell, there was no clergy to convince, nor family against whom to struggle. From now on I was forbidden to act.

The only true freedom that I had left was to speak interiorly to Christ. Otherwise, no doubt, I would never have experienced such a heart-to-heart dialogue.

And so I had the sense that I was becoming very close to him, without my ordeal detracting in any way from that intimate encounter. On the contrary, the difficulties that I overcame only reinforced my attachment to the Son of God, who was suffering also, and who thus became my sole support and my only strength.

But the practice of prayer, even interior prayer, was not easy in the midst of my cellmates. During the day I was always afraid of being discovered while murmuring a Hail Mary or making the sign of the cross as discreetly as possible. This happened to me once in front of one of the detainees, to my great horror, although fortunately he did not understand the meaning of the gesture.

Therefore I made use of the night instead to pray, begging to live long enough to be baptized and to receive Communion. What made me persevere was the certainty, against all human appearances, that one day I would have a right to that privilege.

The months passed and taught me to take ever greater liberties in pursuing this exploration. This interior dialogue even led me sometimes to bold speculations, in which I saw this solitude as a school of faith, a training center for soldiers of Christ.

I imagined that I was there as a convalescent, to be cured of the sickness of not knowing Christ. In my case that sickness had a very precise name: Islam, which authorized me to kill or to lie for my faith. Thanks to the prison it seemed to me that I was recovering spiritual health: things that I had not valued before—peace, meekness—now became essential virtues for me.

At the same time my physical health kept declining as a result of the deplorable hygiene. Although I ate little, I did not sleep that much more. With sixteen in the room, we took turns so that each one could lie down a bit and try to fall asleep. The rest of the time I was standing, a very uncomfortable position in the long run. The slightest movement to stretch my limbs could have bothered my neighbor.

Except that from the start, I had located at the end of the room one unoccupied space: a very low wall that barely masked the corner where we relieved nature. Of course the stench was terrible, but it was the only somewhat isolated place in the room. At night, therefore, I remained standing or crouching on that little wall, slightly apart from the group, which allowed me to pray more easily.

In these very troublesome conditions, month followed month in the dismal repetition of the days, without anything disturbing my interminable wait. What could I expect? I had nothing to hope for, neither a fair trial nor any change in the conditions of my imprisonment. This total absence of prospects was what wore me down the most, even more than the physical torture. Then there was something to struggle against. But how could I fight against the time that was passing?

Through the little window I could just perceive the passport bureau. I spent long hours contemplating the outside of that building, dreaming that it was transformed into a hospital in which the sick would be well attended, with one person to a room.

The only distraction in our dismal days was the weather, the subject of our daily commentaries. I had been there for nine months now, and we had experienced the stifling temperatures of the summer, then, very briefly, the cold of winter. With the month of April there were signs of the returning heat, which was perhaps even more difficult to endure than frost, since our cell was so crowded.

One day, while running my hand around my neck to wipe off the perspiration, I felt something abnormal, a rather voluminous swelling at the base of my neck.

It was not painful but it worried me. I could tell that I was not in good health. After two or three days of procrastinating I noticed also that I had difficulty breathing. When the infirmarian, who went by two or three times a week shouting, came near our cell to find out whether anyone was sick, I told him anxiously that number 318 asked to consult the prison physician.

"It must be [the] thyroid", the man in the white shirt announced to me indifferently while I was putting my clothes back on.

"Is it serious?"

"There will have to be some additional X-rays."

I learned no more about it, despite my insistence.

The man walked me back to the door and told me that I would be taken to the hospital in the coming days. Increasingly concerned about my health, I was of course obliged to seek medical treatment, even though the practitioner at the prison inspired only limited confidence.

In the corridor I noted a bit of information that was not reassuring as I stepped on the scale: now I weighed fifty kilograms [110 pounds]. I had weighed 120 kilos [265 pounds] before setting foot in that penitentiary. I was only a shadow of my former self.

When the day arrived they blindfolded me. An armored wagon transported me to the nearest medical facility.

If I had had any hope of more humane treatment at the hospital, I was rather quickly disillusioned. In order to go inside they made me keep my blindfold on and they wrapped me in a blanket to disguise my identity from indiscreet looks. Even while sick I was still a convict who must not have any contact with the free world.

My two prison guards, moreover, made sure that everyone obeyed that order: they demanded in no uncertain terms to be present at every stage of my medical treatment, and I was under orders not to ask any question of the caregivers. If I needed to communicate I was to do so through the medium of my guard.

The anxiety connected with the examinations and the uncertainty about my condition was thus increased by the pressure of being watched constantly and of having my least actions and gestures supervised—including the operating room where they finally brought me.

Upon entering it, I was paralyzed with fear, but I was not the only one. The hospital personnel, too, it seemed, did not tolerate well this constant pressure right before an operation.

Suddenly the accumulated tension burst forth: the surgeon, exasperated by the presence of the two policemen, firmly ordered them to leave the room. "Anyway, he will be under general anesthesia; it will be as though he were dead", he declared to them with the authority of a practicing physician.

It did not matter; my two guards remained inflexible.

For my part, the words "as though" plunged me into abysmal reflections. I did not know exactly what the operation would consist of, nor the risks involved in the intervention, nor the gravity of my illness. I felt that I had been reduced to the status of a thing, without a word of comfort to alleviate my anxiety, because of the security requirements.

When I regained consciousness, I scarcely had time to emerge from my artificial sleep before they brought me, still teetering, to the armored wagon. Destination: prison.

As I took up residence again in my poor cell, I allowed myself to be overcome with bitterness, perhaps for the first time in my incarceration. The brief stay at the hospital was one trial too many. It became unbearable for me to endure such injustice any longer.

As I chewed on my rancor, I could not help tracing the chain of causes that had brought me there. I had fallen seriously ill because of this beastly prison and its inhumane treatment, to which I had been subjected by the cruelty of my own family, the origin of my misfortune. They had had me incarcerated without any regret, without an ounce of pity.

Deep down, as I thought about them, my brothers, my father especially, I felt profound anger, which consumed me and which nothing could appease.

Moreover, I was enormously concerned about my own family: how were they? Where were my two children, Azhar, the older one, and Miamy, who must have grown a lot? How had my wife reacted to this situation? What had become of them? I had been without any news for so long.

These were the questions that haunted me during those summer months in the stifling heat, when we suffocated while listening distractedly to the noises that ran through the corridors. Through new detainees who replaced those who were gone, we learned that the United Nations had ordered an investigation into al-Hakimieh prison. Saddam Hussein, in fact, had always maintained that there was not one political prisoner in his country and that the opposition was not muzzled.

After sixteen months of captivity I was at the end of my rope. It was the longest and cruelest ordeal that I had ever had to experience. My resistance had been reduced to nothing by so many privations, anxieties, and physical and moral sufferings. I could not bear the idea of spending one more day in that hell.

Hell ended up rejecting me.

One day when I was complaining of my suffering to Christ, in a final supplication, the guards called for number 318. Like a sleepwalker I got up and stepped mechanically, head down, toward the exit. If it was a new session of torture that awaited me, I would not endure it, I was convinced of that. It would be the end. I resigned myself to dying in that way, without resistance, worn out.

Instead of that, the guards held out to me a pile of clothes, mine, which were more than a year old.

"You are free!"

I did not believe my ears.

After all the time spent waiting for that moment, it came so suddenly that I could hardly believe it. It seemed to me unreal to leave my situation as a prisoner so abruptly, to find myself thrown back into the free world. Free.

The only formality was that I sign a paper in which I promised never to reveal what I had experienced, under pain of death—thus, officially, that hell had never existed. The final punishment [was that] even the reality of the ordeal was taken away from me.

The heavy iron door closed behind me. I found myself alone, outside the prison, on that large square exposed to the wind from every direction. Suddenly I was afraid. I was swimming in my clothes; I was just skin and bones. I did not know what to do with this rediscovered freedom.

A Sad Celebration

October 1998

When I had been imprisoned, one year and four months earlier, I had fifteen hundred dinars in my pocket. Today that sum had lost much of its value because of inflation. It was still enough, though, to buy myself a pack of cigarettes and to reflect on my new situation.

I was confronted with a terrible dilemma. I was dying to see my wife and children again, to hold them in my arms, to receive their affection, which I had been cruelly deprived of during my incarceration.

But of course that implied returning to the Musawi clan, visiting those who had handed me over, without being able to yell at them, to tell them of my suffering, or to express the hatred for them that I had accumulated day by day. And I was not sure that I was capable of that.

Just before being set free, I had imagined fleeing to the North and taking refuge in a Christian village and never leaving it—so as not to experience again the interior exile within my own clan, and so as not to live a lie. From now on I no longer considered myself one of them; the ties of affection were broken. I could not forget their treachery.

Yes, I felt very strongly that forgiveness was something impossible for me. Only flight [fleeing] would prevent my relations with my brothers and my parents from degenerating into violence.

What was I to do? Did I really have the right to abandon my wife and children; is that what Christ was asking of me? On the other hand, if I closed the book on my old life, I could live elsewhere a Christian life worthy of the name, without having to hide. Didn't I have the right to hope finally for a bit of rest and tranquility?

I turned these questions over in my mind for almost two hours while smoking one cigarette after another. Torn, I weighed the two options that presented themselves to me, without arriving at a decision.

Finally, after having tormented my mind and having vacillated from one choice to the other, the desire to see my children again was what outweighed all other considerations. I could never be in peace if I abandoned them, left in the odious power of my clan—not to mention that they would certainly not be able to continue practicing their Christian faith. Anwar, Azhar, and my little Miamy would be obliged to return to Islam. And I could not bear that.

So I summoned all the courage that I had left and hailed a taxi, telling the driver to take me home. I did not even have enough money to pay for the fare. But given the extent to which I was going to throw myself again into the maw of the wolf, it seemed to me the least of the torments that awaited me.

Actually I did not have to worry so much about how I was going to find the money that I needed. As we arrived near the house, I recognized one of my brothers, Ali, at the side of the road. I told the taxi driver to stop. There was even a malicious pleasure in taking advantage of the element of surprise to leave to my brother the trouble of paying the driver.

As for me, I traveled on foot the hundred meters [109 yards] that separated me from my family.

While walking, I dreaded the moment of meeting Anwar again as much as I desired it. In more than a year many things must have happened. In prison I had plenty of time to sketch the bleakest scenarios: under my father's pressure had she cracked and admitted our new faith? Didn't that explain the stop of the interrogations after three months of imprisonment?

Would she even recognize me now that I was so thin? This question haunted me as I opened the door of the house that we called our own. The skeletal man that I had become did in fact provoke an initial movement of revulsion in Anwar. I read the surprise on her face. Then her features were lit up by a smile when she finally recognized me. But I hardly had time to take her in my arms.

Suddenly, behind my back, I heard the shouts of a large number of people, a crowd that was forming outside, with the firm intention of entering. I stiffened, fearing the worst, in other words, a repetition of the events of sixteen months ago, when my brothers had assaulted me early in the morning.

Ready to flee, I was nevertheless astonished by the tone of the exclamations, which resembled cheerfulness rather than shouts of hatred. And indeed, I was obliged to move aside for that joyous troop, composed of my extended family, the women ululating, the men surrounding me and embracing me warmly.

I could not understand it at all. Was I hallucinating? If so, my wife seemed to be under the same spell, stupefied by this ebullient reception, which she apparently had not expected either.

Very soon the music started, and my brothers, sisters, and parents were joined [not only] by my in-laws, but also by neighbors and friends. Word had been sent to the whole neighborhood, it seemed, no doubt by my brother, to celebrate my return. Between two shots of a rifle, I was treated to an unending series of embraces, acclamations, and even tears—along the lines of "here at last is our dear son who has returned!" I could not believe my eyes. But I did not have a lot of time to wonder about the significance of the celebration.

For it was indeed a celebration, an even finer one than at my wedding! The house was full of company. In no time they killed several fatted calves to feed the guests. My father had prepared things well.

I no longer had a lot of filial respect for him, but I still gave him credit for one thing: he knew how to make others obey him and to plan expensive events with a masterly hand. Furthermore, he, Fadel-Ali, much more than I, was the center of the gathering, which grew larger with every minute. People crowded around him to congratulate him on the return of his son; they brought him presents. As for me, I was at his side; I smiled at everyone, but deep inside I wanted to weep.

What was this, playacting? A comedy in poor taste, or worse? Had my whole family been stricken with amnesia? Was it possible that they were really and sincerely rejoicing about my return, whereas they ought instead to have feared my revenge? Haunted by these unanswered questions, I passed through the merrymaking as an observer, without experiencing any of the feelings that I simulated, my heart heavy. It lasted until morning and then began again the next day with the arrival of new guests, and the following day as well, until the supplies were exhausted.

I ended up being disgusted by such extravagance. All that for what? To keep up a vile masquerade? But since I had no desire either to dig up the painful past, which had mortified me so much, I remained mute and pretended to take my place in the clan.

That, no doubt, was what they expected of me, I finally realized: that I should take my place in this fine tableau of a family that was reunited at last after a great trial.

Through the snatches of conversation around me, I reconstructed bit by bit the line of the official story, the one that they told to anyone who was willing to commiserate with them. The story of a terrible mistake, the story of a favorite son captured by the secret police in place of another one, as unfortunately happens under the reign of terror inaugurated by Saddam.

But behind the white lie I discerned something else that pained me even more. What ultimately mattered to them, to my father, was their reputation, what people would say, the fear of losing face, much more than mutual love.

That is what had guided their reactions from the start, their unprecedented violence toward me: their preoccupation with camouflaging my conversion to Christianity and suppressing the scandal in good Shiite society, if, in the worst-case scenario, the matter ever became known.

I was astounded—I, who had naïvely thought that I was the beneficiary of some small measure of my relatives' affections. But no—the main thing for them was how things looked externally.

At the same time there was at least one good thing about this realization: the scales fell from my eyes one after the other. I finally saw these people as they really were, in their barefaced cruelty. It was not a pretty sight, but it was the sad reality, I told myself in sorrow and anger.

I also came to understand the reason for my imprisonment and those abominable tortures, from which my body still suffered so much. They had to make me declare the names of the Christians who had welcomed me so as to release me from all culpability and thus to preserve the honor of the family, always that precious reputation, more important than anything else—it nauseated me.

Probably, all those Christians would have been killed then, which by the same token would have prevented me from

ever entering a church again. Among my new coreligionists, too, I would have been a traitor. The plan was not so
badly designed after all.

No doubt it was the death of my cousin Hassan, which
I learned about by chance during those discussions, that
explained why the plan capsized. As a member of the secret
service, he must have been the one who had connived in
those muscular interrogations of which I was the victim.
His sudden death, three months after my incarceration, had
therefore signaled the end of the tortures, a reason that I
could not have suspected at the time, from the depths of
my cell.

Only at the end of those long festivities could Anwar and I
finally be alone together so as to resume our life as husband
and wife. Now, when I say "alone", that is not quite accu-
rate. Once the guests had left, my brother Ali and my sister
Shayma stayed as a protective measure. That was the extent
of the trust that my loving family had for me now.

It was therefore in a low voice, in our bedroom, that we
whispered our confidences to one another. I told her my
story as it really took place, my kidnapping, the ayatollah,
the prison, the hospital.

The further I went in my account, the more upset she
looked. Therefore she had never been informed of the truth.
In turn, Anwar confirmed for me the version about the
judicial error against which nobody could do anything. "Too
bad", they would tell her with a sigh.

"I understand better now", she sobbed to me, "why your
father, with all his fortune and contacts, did not manage to
have his favorite son set free."

During all those long months she found my father passive (not one of his usual characteristics), not taking much
trouble to get me out of there. She had ended up thinking

that I was dead but that no one had the courage to tell her for fear of upsetting her. "Think of it, what hypocrisy! It is worse than anything that I could imagine; I feel deeply betrayed, manipulated, humiliated."

During that time, therefore, Anwar had been confined to her home. In our culture, a wife does not go out without her husband. If her husband is in prison, she herself is imprisoned also, in a way, in her own house. It was also at that moment that my brother and sister had moved into our house, supposedly to assist my wife during her ordeal.

Anwar, who was no fool, found it very difficult to live with that constant surveillance by her in-laws. When she expressed the desire to go spend a few days with her mother, my father granted her permission, provided that she left with him his grandson, Azhar, of whom he was very fond. Indeed, he was the first and only male among all his grandchildren. As a sign of that privilege, he gave my son a large agricultural estate at his birth.

For her part, Anwar trembled the moment her four-year-old son disappeared from her sight. So as to avoid being separated from him, she resigned herself to not leaving the house. Her mother was the one obliged to come and see her to console her.

Even more distressing for my wife was the fact that my father often called for his beloved grandson, wishing to spend time together with him. My brothers, too, sought to have Azhar come visit them regularly. And unfortunately Anwar could not say no to that. Her duty was to comply with every order coming from a man.

Feeling that pressure that the clan was exerting on her, without knowing the reason for it, my wife had the good sense to conceal her prayer life. Her devotions became more discreet and solitary. She no longer dared to read the little Gospel book [Bible] printed on very fine paper that Abouna

Gabriel had given her, for fear of being caught in the act.
She had even sewn it inside her mattress so that no one
would find it.

In retrospect I approved of that prudent decision. But
she felt guilty; she was ashamed of having been so weak as
to conceal her faith in the depths of her soul, for fear of
losing her son. During those long months, Anwar had the
feeling that the flame of her love for Christ was vacillating,
that it was on the point of vanishing for lack of sustenance.
By chance, she confided to me, "The fire did not go out
completely. There were still moments when it warmed my
heart in its trials."

Anger and resentment against my family were not the only
things that agitated Anwar's heart now. When she told me,
shivering, everything that had happened during my absence,
I also perceived in my wife another feeling, an uneasiness,
like a wound caused by irrational fear.

If they were capable of shaming and manipulating others
to that extent, she must have been thinking, how far would
they be ready to go? Would they even endanger the lives of
us all?

"You should know", she added out loud, like an echo
of my own reflections, "that your family took advantage
of our position of weakness to confiscate our identity
papers—along with all the money that we had before your
imprisonment."

So there we were, reduced to a very precarious situation of
financial dependence. The ordinary expenses of day-to-day
life were the responsibility of one of my father's servants.
And as for more important purchases, I was dependent on
the goodwill of the clan. It severely injured my pride, but
it was also very uncomfortable.

Without money it was impossible to make the slightest plan. We would always be under the control of my tribe, at the mercy of the slightest ill will or denunciation, obliged to watch ourselves constantly. The monitoring would never end, not even under my own roof; we would be spied on perpetually by my father's watchdogs.

In those circumstances, there was no point in hoping to resume our trips to Baghdad for Sunday Mass, unless we were willing to take thoughtless risks. The least suspicion about our practice of a religion other than Islam would immediately lead to disaster.

At all costs I had to regain a modicum of freedom, and that meant first of all our financial independence.

Before being imprisoned I had loaned money to some of my father's farm workers, as well as to my brothers. So I turned at first to them. But with each attempt I invariably ran into a brick wall: "Everything is subject to the authority of Fadel-Ali."

Another route was that of the family bus and its driver, which formerly had been a source of income for me from the sale of tickets. Here again I was annoyed to learn that one of my brothers was now the beneficiary of that extra pay. Even the driver, before whom I humbled myself by asking him to lend me some money, enjoyed the luxury of refusing!

If the servants of the family had such arrogance, it was because they had been authorized by Fadel-Ali. I had lost his trust, and with it all the power and the resources that it had conferred upon me.

Refusing to let it discourage me, I resolved to plead my cause to my father.

"Why do you want money?" he asked me drily when I presented my request to him.

"I want to be able to go for a drive with my family, to recover from the prison."

"Come back in two days, and I will see what I can do."

I was counting a bit on the pity and remorse that he may have been feeling for having made me endure so many insults.

But two days later my father proudly announced that he had bought me a house farther away from Baghdad, so that all four of us could settle down there. Nevertheless, he made sure to explain that the house had been put in the name of my older brother rather than in mine. That way there would be no chance of my reselling it.

I was furious: "It's not a house that I need, but money!" I replied by way of thanks, my voice full of rage.

My father was hardheaded. He remained unyielding, and I was obliged to turn on my heels, with my head down.

Six months passed in that way, in that heavy atmosphere of suspicion. I definitely felt that my least gesture was being watched, my comings and goings examined under a magnifying glass. In short, it gave me the impression of being once more in a prison, without bars, but just as efficient.

With one accord Anwar and I decided not to tempt the devil. We refrained for the moment from returning to church. It would be too dangerous for us, with our two inspectors in the house—dangerous also for the Christians, whom we would risk compromising.

It was a very painful period in our life. Externally we tried to put Ali and Shayma on the wrong track by acting in everyday matters as though everything were developing for the best. Interiorly we were experiencing real torment, having to hush up and carefully disguise the things that mattered most to us. I sometimes had the impression that I was a fugitive in hostile territory.

But I worried also that this stressful situation might lead, in my wife's case or mine, to an uncontrolled explosion.

In order to make that intolerable pressure livable, we fortunately had recourse to prayer, which we whispered during our sleeping hours because of our mistrust of our own son! We had been reduced to that. Every night, in a low voice, we begged the Holy Spirit on our knees to help us to carry that burden and to show us a way out, whereas from a human perspective the horizon was completely obstructed.

II

THE EXODUS

"The Church Asks You to Leave"

Summer of 1999, Baghdad

With record-breaking heat in the summer months, the senses became more sluggish, prostrated by temperatures rising to 45°C [113°F]. Was I the one mistaking my desires for reality? I had the feeling that our two guardians were relaxing their surveillance a wee bit.

I deliberately absented myself for increasingly long intervals, without it seeming to rouse them from their torpor. They scarcely opened an eye when I returned at siesta time.

Emboldened by this new freedom, I decided, after mature reflection, to try my luck by going to see Abouna Gabriel. When I told my wife, she trembled with terror. She begged me repeatedly not to go, citing the danger that it entailed for her and the children.

But I was determined and would not relent. We had reached an impasse, and I absolutely had to find a way out of that situation. I strongly felt that with time my anger was growing, faster than my fear, and it was fed by this daily contact with my family, to whom I could not say what was really in my heart.

Despite my prayers for peace of mind, I was becoming more and more irritated by the arrogant attitude of my brothers, who now regarded me as though I were less than nothing. If I did not want them to push me over the edge, I had to act—and flee. I still had a plan that tormented me: to go away and live in a Christian village in the North, which I would never leave again. But how could I flee, and with whom? First I needed to take counsel, and I knew that Abouna Gabriel would be able to listen to me.

Despite my impatience, I nevertheless had taken the time to reflect on several precautions to discourage anyone from following me and so as not to be spotted. Having left at the wheel of my little car, I parked it in the center of the old city before taking a taxi.

And to thwart once again any attempt to track my movements, I asked the driver to cruise through the city for an hour. Only then did I get off at the friary. In normal circumstances it would have taken me scarcely a quarter of an hour, but since I was risking my life, it did not seem excessive to me.

When I arrived at the friary, I found Abouna Gabriel emerging from his siesta, his face still beaming, although he was half-asleep.

"What a surprise! It has been so long."

"Almost two years, Abouna."

"I was worried," he told me, "but I had no way of getting news from anyone."

Our reunion was rather brief. I did not want to awaken suspicion by unduly prolonging the first escape that I attempted. Right away I told him about my imprisonment and then about why I had not come since then.

The old priest did not seem to be surprised: "Your parents' reaction is on the whole quite normal in a Muslim society. Do not forget that the Qur'an prescribes the death penalty for those who try to leave Islam. But you should not have taken books home with you."

"Can I come back to church?" I begged him anxiously.

"The church is open for you, but now you must redouble your prudence."

There was no need to tell me that. I pressed my advantage, relying on his good disposition.

"And could we resume our discussion as before, twice a week?"

Abouna Gabriel agreed with a nod. He looked at me for a long time, with that kindness that had always calmed me. Today, though, there was an unaccustomed seriousness in it.

I left the friary lighthearted and confident, for the first time in months. The support of the friar and his kindliness reassured me. It was a rock in the midst of so many trials.

Encouraged by this initial success, Anwar and I perfected a stratagem to frustrate the efforts of our guardians at home: the recurring argument. This was not conveyed by abusive language, as is commonly the case, but by gestures, or rather by the absence of gestures. In our little scenario, my wife refused to play the good, devoted spouse, by forgetting, for example, to serve me a meal!

Curiously, our conflicts occurred practically every week, preferably on Saturday, and inevitably concluded in the same way: Anwar went back to her mother's house! I was therefore obliged, reluctantly, to take the car to go find her. And thus I had an excellent cover to go with her to Mass. Sometimes the pouting lasted several weeks, which allowed us to go and meet our spiritual director together.

Our relatives were hoodwinked. Better yet, they proved to be so preoccupied by this apparent conflict that the members of my family became obliging, overwhelming Anwar with attentions to encourage her to take better care of her husband.

One evening, after three months of employing this ruse assiduously, Abouna Gabriel abruptly concluded one of our discussions with this recommendation: "You must come less often; it is too dangerous, for you as well as for us. Come only once a week, in addition to Mass."

I did not know how to interpret this admonition, but I complied, not really having any choice. Maybe it was wisdom being expressed through the words of Abouna. In any case, it certainly lessened the danger that our family would one day see through our ploy.

Several weeks later, [there was] a new warning from the priest: "From now on you can come only once a week. Therefore you have to choose between Mass and our meetings." Here again there was no appeal. I chose Mass, but it was heartrending to have to give up those evenings that were so full of spiritual lessons.

This time Abouna Gabriel's instructions caused me to reflect. He could not have made that decision on his own initiative. That was not like him. Why would he have stepped back, once he had accepted in principle our regular meetings? He was not a man to speak lightly. Therefore there must have been some other reason. He lived in a friary, and the odds were that his brothers in religion had become frightened of the danger.

It was also possible that the Massgoers on Sunday, informed by an indiscretion of one of the friars, had become alarmed at the presence of a Muslim in the congregation—and for fear of being accused of proselytism, had put pressure on the religious community. I recalled now a little detail to which I had paid no attention, but which had registered on my memory: for several weeks now it had seemed to me that the faces of the people at Mass had fallen the moment we made our entrance into the church.

[There was a]nother troubling coincidence: Anwar and I noticed that the security had been reinforced; we saw that the entrance to the church was now patrolled by parishioners who were responsible for spotting strangers and potential spies. That was a sign that the risk had increased, and our presence was very probably the cause.

I could understand these fears and the reasons for them: the harshness of Muslim Sharia law, the risks for the whole community—and in a certain way I shared them. But I did not feel that I was showing great imprudence by coming there—especially since my thirst for Christ was so great that it allowed me to overcome such apprehension.

I felt as though I was being carried along by an irrepressible impulse that swept away the objections and the obstacles and was concentrated on one goal: baptism, and even more, communion with "the bread of life". It is difficult to explain, but sometimes I thought that I was being protected by a supernatural force that I did not possess within myself. Having survived all those ordeals gave me a sense of invulnerability, although I realized that this also involved some measure of pride. In any case it was this apparent unawareness that drove me to continue my quest, to hope that there was a way out of this situation, somewhere, and that I just had to search persistently.

With a bit of condescension, I was also surprised at those believers who were paralyzed with fear. To me it seemed almost incompatible with the saying of Christ that had struck me: "Do not fear those who kill the body but cannot kill the soul" (Mt 10:28).

One Sunday at the end of Mass, Abouna Gabriel signaled to me to join him in the sanctuary. He made an appointment with me for the following Wednesday before going back to the sacristy to remove his vestments.

For three days, astonished by this unusual way of proceeding, I oscillated between joy at being able to spend another evening with that priest, for whom I had a great deal of affection, and apprehension: the fear of finding out this time that I was forbidden to come to church.

On the appointed day, I realized the seriousness of the moment when Abouna Gabriel had me enter his room and immediately closed the door behind me.

"What I am about to say to you must not leave here", he announced to me by way of a preface. "You must promise me that you will not tell anyone."

Disconcerted by this enigmatic way of broaching the subject, I kept silent, my stomach in knots, waiting for what he would say next.

"You are not baptized, but you are a true Christian, no doubt much more so than I and a good number of others here", he continued. "But when you are a Christian, you must obey Christ. And Christ's representative on earth is the Church."

"Well?" I asked, with a horrible presentiment, imploring him not to mince words.

"In the name of the Church, for prudence's sake, I order you to leave Iraq."

I remained motionless for several seconds, my eyes fixed on that venerable man. He had just calmly commanded me to draw the bottom line under my entire life. It was a rude shock. Even during the darkest times of the last few years, never had I thought of going away. It seemed to me that I was like Abraham, whom God told to leave everything— except that I had no money, and no occupation either.

"Can we discuss this? Is this negotiable?"

"No," Abouna Gabriel firmly replied, "if you resist this order, you resist the Church!"

The argument had its effect. The clergyman knew it. At the mere idea of setting myself against the Church, even for a moment, I was terrified.

That would call into question everything for which I had fought for twelve years. I had not sought so energetically to be admitted to the Church—and God knows that I had paid dearly—only to enjoy now the luxury of disdaining a single one of her orders.

Moreover, this order did not come from just anywhere. It was delivered to me by a man whom I revered more than any other, who had followed my journey step by step. Therefore I could have confidence: the order that was being given to me today must be the fruit of mature reflection. It explained, at any rate, why Abouna Gabriel had insisted that we meet less frequently.

From now on I no longer had a choice. I had to comply. But I still needed time—just a little breathing space so as to digest all this information, to reflect on the new hand that was being dealt to me.

"You have a week", the old friar explained to me. "In seven days you will tell me whether your answer is yes or no. If it is yes, the universal Church will help you. But if it is no, then you must never again come to see me and you must renounce baptism."

"I know no other country", I asserted timidly.

"Well, I have traveled a lot", he replied eagerly. "I can advise you. But you are the one who will decide. I love you immensely, you know, and if something happened to you in Iraq, I would never get over it. You are my dearest friend!"

At those words I felt the tears filling my eyes, for in our discussions Abouna Gabriel had always been careful to minimize the emotional component, cutting short any outbursts of affection. But that evening, perhaps one of the last, I noted with emotion that he had not been able to restrain his words. He had let his heart speak. That consoled me somewhat for the uprooting that I now had to prepare for.

As I returned home, I was very apprehensive about my wife's reaction, since she was extremely fearful. How could I help her to decide, when I myself was half-convinced? If I refused to follow Abouna Gabriel's command, I could stop calling myself a Christian. But the thought of traveling made me terribly uneasy, if only about our livelihood. Without a profession, without a diploma, how could I feed my family?

What I dreaded most, ultimately, was to find myself in the most humiliating condition of all: that of a refugee. In my head I had images of Palestinian refugees receiving food like dogs. And I was not ready to accept that—just as it was difficult for me to accept the idea of living in someone else's house and depending on outside support.

I should have expected it; Anwar's first reaction was negative. She could not work either; we were accustomed to a household that was permanently run by domestic servants, including the kitchen. And then there were the children, Azhar and Miamy, aged seven and two-and-a-half, respectively. For my wife it was unthinkable that our flight would go unnoticed if we took our little ones along.

By dint of turning the problem around in every direction, one fact at least became clear: our present situation was untenable, inasmuch as we both hoped to be baptized. Therefore the most important thing was not to panic and to calm our fear of the unknown.

So as to leave no stone unturned, Anwar decided after a few days to try one last time to reason with Abouna Gabriel. Pretending to have another argument with me, she left to stay with her family. But this time she traveled alone to see the friar, leaving her children with her mother and saying that she was going to see her sister, without specifying which one.

As she arrived at the friary, she imagined that she could convince Abouna to change his mind. She knew that he had great affection for her, too. Alas, the answer was the same: "There is no other solution. Otherwise it is death for you and a tremendous amount of trouble for the Christian community."

When the seven-day respite had passed, and our hopes of an alternative had evaporated, I in turn went back to see the priest to give him my answer:

"Yes. But . . .", I hesitated. "I do not want to be a refugee!"

"In that case, why don't you take out a loan?" Abouna Gabriel suggested to me, after reflecting for a while.

"To me that is still being dependent; I want nothing of it!"

"You will find work", he concluded, urging me to trust.

Secret Preparations

Baghdad, January 2000

As the new year began, I set about preparing methodically for our departure, praying also that the steps I was taking would be as discreet as possible.

First I had to obtain passports for us. To do that, I needed a birth certificate and an identity card—documents confiscated by my family. I also lacked a certificate of nationality, especially one specifying our degree of nationality. This is a difficult document to obtain, especially without a birth certificate. It certifies that a person is an Iraqi of good stock, by birth or by marriage.

Fortunately I had kept on my person proof that I had completed my military service. It was an obligatory document, which serves as proof of identity. I had to be able to present it at any moment to the police, on the slightest pretext. Today it would help me to reconstitute the required certificates.

It so happened that my family had no contact with the government. The clan had rather defiant relations with it, considering it a tool of Saddam Hussein. Therefore there was no a priori risk that an indiscretion might compromise my efforts.

On the other hand, having been burned once by the episode with the Bible, I scrupulously made sure not to leave any official paper at the house, for fear that my watchdogs might find it. They were all with Abouna Gabriel for safekeeping. Another necessary precaution was that I refused for the moment to let my wife accompany me as I made preparations, so as not to arouse suspicions.

Painful experience had taught me that I had to mistrust everyone, especially my relatives, and so I was constantly on my guard. For prudence's sake, I made sure not to let more than one or two days go by—never more than a week—without going to see my father, for whatever reason. I was all the more vigilant because in order to leave the family fiefdom, I had to take the road that runs past my father's house.

What saddened me was that my father waited until the moment when I was getting ready to leave before trying to get closer to me again. Recently it had seemed to me that he was acting less suspicious of me. How much of that was calculation, and how much was sincere? [It was d]ifficult to say. He may have been afraid of me, suspecting that I wanted vengeance. In that case it was better for him to cajole me than to confirm me in my role as victim.

Nevertheless, I also sensed very strongly that he hoped to restore our confidence. I knew that deep down he did love me and would have been devastated to lose me. Of course, that was conveyed without words; he was much too bashful and proud to tell me so. But his whole attitude, his attentive gestures, showed solicitude, a willingness to reestablish our ties after the rupture of recent years—as though

our happiness in the past had not been destroyed by what
he had made me undergo.

For my part, I had forgotten nothing. Try as I might, I
found it very difficult to disguise my hatred for that family
that had betrayed me [and] handed me over without any
regret and condemned me to the most squalid punishment.

And even if it were possible for me to forgive, how could
I ever explain to them what I was going through now? To
me it seemed impossible; my religious experience was so
far beyond the scope of their understanding.

After obtaining passports, the second major difficulty was pack-
ing our bags. Here again I had to act with the utmost discretion. Naturally it was unthinkable to gather up our things at
our house, right under the noses of our prison guards. So as
not to attract attention, I planned to carry them away piece-
meal, in a little backpack that I always wore on my errands.
Every time I left the house, the backpack allowed me to carry
out one piece of clothing and to leave it with Michael, who
agreed to let his house serve as a cloakroom on this occasion.

For the trip I bought a large suitcase. Gradually it was
filled up, and after several weeks, it was overflowing. We
would be obliged to sort things before leaving.

Thank God, the disappearance of our clothes went unnoticed. We had managed to keep my brother and sister from
having access to our room and only very rarely left the house
entirely to their indiscretion. Even in the rare cases when
that had happened, it seemed that they had respected our
conjugal intimacy, at least. At any rate, even if they had
dared to go into our room, we had so much stuff that they
would not have noticed the difference!

There was one final question [concern] for me to settle
before our departure, and it was not the least important:

finding money for the journey. I did not know how long our exile would last, and therefore I needed a significant sum in order to subsist. And I had neither income nor assets that I could liquidate.

I thought at first of selling my automobile. But Abouna Gabriel, to whom I confided the plan, advised against it—too tasteless for my family, too risky, as well. I would have to arrange with the buyer that he would not own the car right away, but only on the day of my departure, since I would still need it for my preparations. And that would run the risk of arousing suspicions. And so selling my car to a Muslim was ruled out, but even to a Christian it would have been daring. Since my life was at stake, I preferred to forget that plan.

I had only one other way to raise some money: Anwar's jewelry, which she offered to me spontaneously. I hesitated. I myself would never have dared to ask her for them. Those jewels constituted her personal fortune, her only property. In general, Muslim women are often quite attached to their jewelry, because it is the only thing that they are allowed to own.

I was well aware that in offering them to me freely, she was placing into my hands much more than money. Anwar was thus signaling her total commitment to this plan to leave, despite all the risks that it involved. My wife had made a choice between the Calvary that our life among our relatives had become and the road to exile. In bringing me her jewelry, she delicately added a remark that convinced me to accept her offer: "You know, these jewels are not more precious in my sight than the love of Jesus. It is not too big a sacrifice to make for him."

Even if I would have to buy her some costume jewelry to replace them, the sale of the real ones nevertheless brought a considerable sum, around ten thousand dollars. That is far from the real value of those jewels—I was in a hurry and the buyer took advantage of the situation, but it allowed me to look a bit more serenely toward the future.

On the other hand, it was all that I could do to convince Anwar not to try to bring her superb tableware, to which she was very much attached. I had to employ infinite patience and repeated explanations to persuade her that we could not possibly overload ourselves.

Four months later, after long preparations, we were almost ready to depart.

After doing my research, I had chosen Jordan as our destination, because it was the only country that had not closed its borders with Iraq. The new king, Abdullah II, was an ally of the West, and refugees were an appreciable source of revenue for that country; only the richest people had the means with which to flee Saddam's dictatorship.

All that was left for me to do was to retrieve the family passport [for which I had applied] and to determine the date of our flight. For the moment everything seemed to be going as well as possible; it was almost miraculous that my family had not noticed anything.

On the appointed day Anwar and I staged a new argument, and we went as a family, with the children, as the government requires, to pick up the precious document.

The disappointment was proportionate to our feverish expectation: the official announced to me in a neutral tone of voice that I did not have the right to travel.

It was a terrible blow. Within the space of ten seconds I imagined myself lost, thrown behind bars for the rest of my life. I was desperate. It was surely a matter of treachery on the part of my family. They had foreseen everything, even the possibility of self-exile on my part. I must have been denounced to the government while I was in prison, when my cousin in the secret service was still alive.

Although I was upset, I managed to speak a few words, the last hope of a condemned man: "What can I do?" The response was cold. "Your only option is to file a claim in the office next door."

Suddenly, as I listened, I saw a glimmer. I remembered that corruption is an extremely widespread reality in the Iraqi government, especially since inflation has undermined salaries. I had watched my father in action; I knew that money enables one to obtain many things. Why not this time? It was now or never. Somewhat reassured, I ventured a new question: "Something else. Do you know the reason for this travel ban?"

"Surely you must know?"

"Hmm ... Yes, yes, I remember now. I must have borrowed money from someone without repaying him, but now it is settled; I have paid my debt."

At that moment when my future was at stake, double or nothing, my imagination was working fast! The mention of money, it seemed, caught the attention of my interlocutor.

"Then it is enough for you to go to the police, who can make all the arrangements", the official explained, suddenly becoming conciliatory.

After a moment's hesitation, he continued: "But they will bother you with questions and formalities. If you like, I can take care of it."

There you go. I had guessed right. I then agreed to the official's proposal by asking him the price for this "service".

"A half million dinars", he answered with self-assurance.

An exorbitant sum, which in those days was the equivalent of around four hundred dollars! I made some rapid calculations: he must draw a salary of three thousand dinars monthly; that sum would therefore guarantee him a comfortable retirement. Better to bargain!

After a short discussion, we reached an agreement on a quarter of a million, 250,000 dinars: 150,000 to be paid right away, the rest the following day upon delivery of the passport.

When I left, I made a detour via the friary of Abouna Gabriel and told him about my uneasiness:

"And if tomorrow, when I return, he tells me, 'I do not know you'?"

"Tomorrow we will see", the priest reassured me; "for now we will pray that it goes smoothly. And if not, you can try to flee to the North."

The next day I returned to the office of the civil servant, again with my wife and my two children. I was tense. He presented the passport to me, with the precious official stamp. But as I looked at it more closely, I noticed beside the stamp an enigmatic inscription: "It is not the designated person."

I did not understand the meaning of it. Whatever it was, it was too late to back out. I went outside with the employee so as to give him the remainder of the sum. As we walked away from the building, so as to be discreet, I had a bitter taste in my mouth, the vague feeling that I had just been cheated.

To be sure, I had my exit visa, but what was going to happen to me at the Jordanian border with that odd note? I did not dare to ask him, and anyway I had no choice.

In my plan, Jordan was just one stage. Once established there, I would ask for a visa to a Western country, which was no longer possible here in Iraq: almost all the foreign embassies in Baghdad had packed up and left since the [Persian] Gulf War in 1990.

I had also learned with some dread that sometimes you had to wait for months or even years in Jordan before obtaining a visa. The money was then quickly spent and the Iraqi families were impoverished. I hoped, without any assurance, that our funds would suffice.

As for our final destination, that was unknown. Having no acquaintances abroad, I felt helpless in confronting that distressing question. Then, to overcome my fear, I left that entirely to Abouna Gabriel.

He preferred Italy, where he had a brother who could welcome me. But so as not to overlook any possibility, he also had me meet with a French diplomat, Jean-Pierre Bagaton.

The man arrived at the friary by motorbike, no doubt so as to be more discreet, and spoke Arabic. The diplomat was very kind and helped me to fill out the forms and even proposed, to my great surprise, a visa for France.

Disconcerted, I reflected for a few minutes before declining his offer. Having a French visa on my passport could only serve to arouse the suspicions of the customs officers at the border. Since I was not supposed to leave the country except for a quick round trip, it did not seem very prudent to me.

After that high-ranking French official left, I remained alone for a moment with Abouna Gabriel. It was no doubt one of the last times that I would see him before saying adieu at my departure. Whereas until now he had left me free—a dizzying freedom—in my choice of a future host country, now all of a sudden he was determined:

"You will remain for one night in Jordan, and the next day you will leave for France."

"And . . . what about baptism? The promise that you made to me?"

The burning question had been on the tip of my tongue for a while, but I had never dared to formulate it. But today was different. The prospect of an imminent departure top-pled all my barriers.

The question was direct, and the answer was just as blunt.

"It is too dangerous", he told me. "You will have a won-derful celebration over there."

With those words Abouna Gabriel had just ruined my fondest hope. That was what had made me persevere for so many years; all my efforts had been aimed at that prospect.

And here we were, about to be uprooted, obliged to run away from our lives to an unknown land, without even hav-ing the chance to receive the baptism that we desired so much.

Farewells

Baghdad, April 19, 2000

During those four months of preparation, I had had the time to fine-tune every detail of our escape, while collab-orating closely with Abouna Gabriel, who, in those cir-cumstances, had given me permission to visit him at the friary at any time.

Together we reviewed the different stages with one very clear objective: to get past the constant surveillance of my family, even if it was relaxed. By holding the purse strings tightly, my father supposed that he was controlling me suf-ficiently by means of money, that he no longer had to watch the slightest movement that I made.

Thus I had a somewhat freer hand with which to orga-nize our departure. I subdivided it into four phases, corre-sponding to the four places that would serve as landmarks along our escape route.

Two days previously, my wife had left the house, under the pretext of a new quarrel, so as to be able to go to her family's house and say her wordless good-byes. It was an agonizing ordeal for her. She was obliged to take her leave from them in the secret of her heart, without telling them anything. She would never again attend the large, warm family gatherings on Friday, where all her brothers and sisters loved to meet. She felt like a branch torn away from its tree, she told me.

As one last tie that would henceforth connect her to her family, before leaving she took a scarf belonging to her mother, whom she venerated, and put it on her head. She promised to bring it back the next time.

After paying all the intermediaries, officials, and traffickers, I brought the money that I had left, around four thousand dollars, to Abouna's friary for safekeeping. We had decided together that I would keep two thousand dollars for the journey and that the other half would make its way to Jordan through Church networks. At customs, the maximum allowed was two hundred dollars, just what was needed for a round-trip.

Our baggage was stored at Michael's house, ready to be carried off at the time of our escape. All that remained was the vehicle and its driver, if possible not an Iraqi. After several inquiries I tracked down a taxi driven by a Jordanian; [there was] no chance, therefore, that he might know me. We would meet him in an isolated, discreet place in the city, Al-Mansur, which saw much less traffic than the taxi station in Al-Salhieh.

The day of our departure—hoped for and dreaded at the same time—finally arrived.

In the wee hours of the morning I got into my car. Anxiety weighed on my stomach. I had slept very poorly. I had spent the whole night reviewing in an endless loop the plan for the day to come, trying to detect the flaw that would ruin us.

The sun rose. I was impatient to move on to the active stage of my plan but at the same time terrified as well by the thought of the risk that I was making my family run. If unluckily I was captured, I no longer had any protection at all, no safety net. It was certain death.

If somehow I were to be spared capital punishment, it might be even worse: I would have to endure once more the humiliation of being less than nothing within my clan. Until now I had persevered, thanks to this plan to leave. If it failed, I would not have the strength to put up with that dishonor for another second.

So it was with determination, despite my fear, that I turned the ignition key to go collect my wife and children. From there I drove slowly, constantly watching in the rearview mirror to detect anyone who might be following us, to a parking lot so as to leave my car there and take the first taxi.

In the cab that brought us first to see Abouna Gabriel, the fear was palpable. No one said a word. We physically felt the tension of the hours that awaited us.

Abouna was also very moved by that solemn moment. He took us in his arms, his gestures conveying the gravity of the situation. So as not to burst into tears, he very quickly brought us to the chapel, near the altar of the Blessed Virgin. There we recited together one Hail Mary; the final words echoed strangely in my ears: "Pray for us ... at the hour of our death."

Time was pressing. We said our good-byes to him and promised to send news as soon as possible. The words caught in my throat; we would probably never see him again. As he shook our hands, our dear Abouna gave us one last token of esteem, by confiding in us the story of his religious vocation.

"When I was a child," he said, while placing his hands on the children's heads, "I was very sick. And my mother promised to give me to the Church if I was cured. You, too," the old man added, looking at us in turn, "Anwar, and you, Muhammad, you will ask the Lord for a child, and you will consecrate him to God."

For him this was a way of exorcizing the danger, of invoking divine protection and sending us off into the future, into life, a life that we would lead in peace; at that moment I hoped with all my heart that we would find it at the end of our flight.

Then the priest blessed us and nudged us toward the exit while handing us passports and money. We had to leave. After the time it took to hail a taxi, we were a little more detached from our life here in Baghdad.

In the cab that brought us to Michael's house, I was on the lookout. At every intersection I was afraid of being recognized by my family or by Anwar's relatives. But I knew very well that from now on I could not influence the course of events. In the event of an unlucky encounter, there would be nothing to justify our strange behavior.

To calm my anxiety I could only rely on heaven to bring us safely out of the city. With all my senses alert, I watched the driver out of the corner of my eye. I distrusted everything and everyone during the twenty or so minutes that the trip lasted, minutes that seemed to turn into hours. When we had arrived at Michael's, we all got out of the cab. I waited for the taxi to drive away.

We entered the shop without a word. With a nod Michael brought us into his house, so that we could pick up our suitcases. Then I called another taxi to take us to the fourth point, from which we would finally leave the city.

The good-byes to Michael were short. The young man watched us leave, crowded in the cab, and gave us a friendly wave of his hand. The closer we came to our final rendez-vous, the more at ease I felt. Each stage that was completed removed a weight from me: the weight of fear. But I began to breathe freely only when I saw the Jordanian driver, who was waiting for us at the appointed place.

When the cab finally drove onto the highway that leads to the border, Anwar asked me for a cigarette—the first one in her life. She too had endured the intolerable wait for that moment when we would go beyond the city gates of Baghdad.

We traveled southwest at a lively pace. The hours passed, along with the kilometers. As we traveled farther from Baghdad, my fears returned and focused on the border crossing. What would happen? Would the enigmatic inscription on my passport sign my death warrant?

I gripped uneasily the few hundred dollars that remained. That sum was now all that we had. On it would depend our survival in this country that we knew nothing about. How long would it last us? I preferred not to think about it.

After eight hours on the road, we were approaching the border. I asked the driver to stop at a restaurant—not that we were really hungry, but I thought that we needed to renew our strength and to provide ourselves with what we would need later, since we did not know what awaited us on the other side of the border.

Not one of us had the stomach to swallow even one bite. Anxiety had taken away our appetites. But the stop did us good; we went out of the restaurant loaded down with the wrapped leftovers from the meal that we had scarcely touched.

In the setting sun, finally, the customs post was silhouetted against the horizon. We had been on the road for almost ten hours. Although we were exhausted by the long trip and by our emotions, we still had to overcome this last obstacle in order to begin to feel safe.

Most importantly, we had to pay the official tax that is owed by any Iraqi who wishes to leave the country: four hundred dollars per adult and two hundred per child—a total of twelve hundred dollars.

As I paid that considerable sum, I had no guarantee whatsoever of the result, since the most precarious step came next: the police checkpoint. I trembled at the thought of showing my passport with its fraudulent stamp; to put it mildly, its efficacy appeared dubious to me.

The customs officer inspected the vehicle with a suspicious air, walking all around the exterior and peering at each one of us in turn. Inside, no one moved. Anwar and I held our breath, praying for the children, especially Azhar; they remained seated and well behaved, without opening their mouths.

After completing his inspection, the man signaled for me to get out, with my passport. As I climbed out of the cab I exchanged a frightened look with my wife. My knees were shaking. I knew that that moment was critical: there would be no second chance, and failure meant death.

The keen awareness of being at a point of no return, however, gave me a second wind. It was too late to go back. I assumed an aloof demeanor and handed him my papers. Inside of me, everything was clenched.

Even before glancing at my passport, the customs officer asked my name and typed it on his computer keyboard. I thought that I was already ruined. By leaning slightly over the counter I saw the screen, on which was posted the terrible phrase: "Forbidden to travel". Panic seized me. Unable to make a gesture or to speak a word, I was paralyzed. That notice certainly meant the end of the road for us.

Silently the customs officer kept looking at his computer while distractedly consulting the pages of my passport. My head shrunk down between my shoulders as I waited for the order to arrest us. But the man tranquilly continued his inspection. It was unbearable. He stopped at the visa, looked at the inscription by the official in Baghdad, seemed to reflect for a few interminable seconds, and then handed me the document with a smile.

I was still dumbfounded. It made no sense. Then, suddenly, the light went on; the meaning of the phrase [was] "It is not the designated person." The shady official had managed things well; he thus explained in advance to his colleague at customs that the man on the run who was being sought by the police was not the one presenting the passport. It was simply a case of an identical name.

It was awfully well thought out. In retrospect I mentally smiled in appreciation at that obscure employee, whom I had wrongly suspected of having duped me.

"Would you happen to have something to eat?"

I had been deep in thought, but the customs officer's question brought me to my senses. I smiled in turn. Luck was definitely on our side that evening—unless it was a wink from Providence, who led us to this man who, no doubt, was underpaid and hungry to boot!

"Don't move; I'll be right back!" I said to him jovially by way of an answer.

In the twinkling of an eye, I hurried to bring him all the food, still hot, that we were saving for later. To hell with prudence! I was so happy with the turn of events that I was ready to make any sacrifice—denying my stomach would cost me little.

Astonished at the unexpected abundance, the man did not even think to ask us for money. I was prepared for that possibility, however, because I was not sure that the special note on my passport was entirely proper. Corruption had spread like gangrene through so much of the underpaid government bureaucracy that it had become routine, the norm.

But that evening his appetite was what governed his conduct. He was so distracted that he scarcely glanced at our baggage, which contained valuable objects that we could not have done without.

Just one thing intrigued him, in a final burst of bureaucratic zeal: Why were we bringing so much clothing, if it was for a simple trip from which we would soon return?

Borne up by good humor, I did not let that sudden fit of conscientiousness disconcert me. I offered to give him some of it and added that the presence of the little ones was a proof of our good faith: if we had had the intention of fleeing, we would never have brought children so young on such a dangerous adventure.

This last argument managed to convince our border guard definitively; besides, he was just looking for something to assuage his professional conscience so that he could let us pass his guard post.

As I got back into the cab, I addressed a short prayer of thanksgiving to my guardian angel; we crossed on foot the few meters that still separated us from Jordan.

If my calculations were correct, we had three or four more hours to travel through the desert before arriving in Amman. We drove through the silence of nightfall, meditating on that rough day.

Certainly it was not the promised land, but I felt happy and relieved, like Moses crossing the Red Sea. My anxiety had been reduced by half.

I did not know what the future held; nevertheless, I had the impression that by leaving Iraq I was leaving behind also the severe trials of the past years. The torture, sickness, and sufferings that I had experienced during my imprisonment remained cruelly inscribed on my flesh, but all of that became less acute, further away, and seemed suddenly easier to bear.

Oddly enough, even the deep hatred that I felt for my family seemed diminished now by the distance between us.

The night was pitch-black when we spied the halo of light over the Jordanian capital. I asked our driver to show us an affordable hotel.

Either we did not have the same idea of what constitutes a modest price, or else our man lied to us. He left us at a hotel named "The Palace", where a room is a hundred dollars a night: a small fortune that amounted to one-third of our remaining budget.

But for the moment we were exhausted and unable to argue or to look for another hotel. I put off till tomorrow the search for other lodgings, and we collapsed onto our bed, overwhelmed by fatigue and emotions.

In Exile

Amman, Jordan, April 20, 2000

The next morning I had two objectives in mind for this first day on Jordanian soil: contacting a nun recommended by Abouna Gabriel, and going to the apostolic vicariate of Amman, where I was to retrieve my sum of two thousand dollars.

So I took a taxi to the address noted by Abouna Gabriel. It was a convent of women religious, the old Iraqi priest had explained to me: "Ring the doorbell and ask to speak to Sister Maryam."

I rang, and in response the door opened a little, revealing a distrustful, frightened face belonging to a nun who was no doubt of Philippine origin.

"She is not here. Come back in an hour!" she told me while closing the door quickly.

Probably my bronzed Iraqi face and my corpulence scared her.

I had an hour to wait, and so I decided to go to the apostolic vicariate. But I had no papers on me, no written recommendation, and I announced right off the bat to the receptionist that Abouna Gabriel had sent me and must have left something there for me. Flabbergasted, the secretary looked at me as though I had come from the moon: "We know nothing about that."

Obviously it was not possible for me to offer her any other explanations; I would thereby risk drawing attention to myself immediately.

Vexed by this new setback, I returned to the convent, determined that this time they would open the door.

Meanwhile Sister Maryam had returned and happily agreed to see me. I sensed, however, that the Filipina nun at the entrance only reluctantly opened the door for me; she still seemed a bit scared. She led me through a corridor into a little room where the nun was waiting. About sixty years old, tall and solidly built, the nun looked at me with a resolute, distrustful expression. She did not seem comfortable. But, after all, Abouna Gabriel was the one who had warmly recommended me; I could be confident.

"Sister, I was sent by Abouna Gabriel, and I have a letter for you", I quickly said to her while handing her the safe-conduct, my only significant lead in this country.

There were only a few words on the letter: "Here is a family that you should help." No doubt this was a final precaution taken by Abouna Gabriel; if I were to be arrested, it might constitute proof of charges against me.

"Very well. How can I help you?" the nun asked me energetically, like someone who did not have time to spend on formalities.

Then briefly I told her my story, about my conversion and my reasons for fleeing from Iraq. She listened to me attentively, with concentration. I finished by saying that I was looking for an apartment to rent while we were staying there in Jordan, because the hotel was definitely unaffordable.

When I told her how much the previous night had cost us, she was startled and scandalized: "That is extravagant! You were cheated by your driver, the one who brought you into Jordan. He must be an agent of the hotel owner. That happens rather often here. Refugees are considered milk cows."

Lesson learned, at my expense. I noted also with relief that Abouna Gabriel's recommendation produced its effect: the nun seemed to take to heart the cause of defending and protecting us.

"Did you take a taxi to come here?" she then asked me, suspiciously.

"Yes ... Why?"

"Better to avoid that. It's the best way of being spotted when you are a refugee. For the moment you must be discreet. You never know! How did you pay for the taxi? Do you have money?"

"I have some, but it is at the apostolic vicariate, and I do not know how to retrieve it. All that I have left in my pocket are a few Iraqi dinars. I gave one of them to the taxi driver to bring me here. At this rate, I will not last long."

"You gave a dinar to the taxi driver?" she said suddenly, stopping me in the middle of my explanations.

"That is what I just said, and I told him to keep the change."

To my great surprise she burst out laughing, a hearty, rough laughter, just like her mountaineer's accent. I wondered what was funny about my situation!

"The thing is," she explained with a smile, "one dinar is worth about a thousand fils in Jordanian money—so that you gave the driver more than double the price of a usual trip, which is four hundred fils ... No, really, it is better for you to travel by public transportation; you will be less conspicuous!"

Somewhat annoyed at having been so naïve, I said no more. Sister Maryam seemed to notice my embarrassment and became serious again.

"I will see what I can do about your lodgings. I have an Iraqi Christian friend who may be able to help you."

That afternoon the nun introduced me to Sayid. He lived in a district in the city where houses were not too expensive, a little less than one hundred dinars per month. The Iraqis regrouped there while waiting to obtain a foreign visa, usually to the West, North America or Europe.

As luck would have it, he had heard about a house for rent not far from his place, for sixty-five dinars. "Come see it", he kindly suggested to me. Two hours later the deal was done and the contract with the owner was signed. We could move in that same evening.

One incident, however, disturbed the smooth unfolding of that first day. As I signed the document and Sayid learned that my name was Muhammad, he jumped in alarm and was about to call me to account. How could a Muslim have made his way into a Christian community?

Sister Maryam stopped him, took his arm firmly, and imperiously mouthed the word: "Later!"

I thanked heaven for having introduced me to that nun, who was taking our situation in hand. The same incident made me understand that the situation of Christians in Jordan, although better than in Iraq, was far from being as enviable as I might have imagined.

Playing her role of stalwart guardian angel to the hilt, Sister Maryam accompanied me to the hotel, where I rejoined my wife and children. From there we went shopping together, since the house was empty, and scrounged some mattresses at the convent. They came from well-educated Jordanians, the nun explained to me.

Seeing my astonishment at this unexpected assistance, Sister Maryam told me that she had frequent contacts with Iraqi Christians. She traveled regularly in my country, with other nuns, to catechize the children in the remote Christian villages, so remote, she added, that the little ones got down on the ground at prayer time to do as the Muslims around them do.

But those missions put her in danger. It was quite likely that she was even under surveillance by the Jordanian police. That was why, she admitted to me, she had been afraid when her sisters had reported to her with alarm that a tall Iraqi with a mustache was asking to see her!

In a rather unexpected way, there we were, set up in a permanent residence, a house. That was not at all how I had pictured the fate of refugees—even though in any case the situation was only a temporary one for me. As soon as possible, I was convinced, we would have to leave Jordan.

We were still too close to Iraq. My family surely had not given up so easily on carrying out the fatwa pronounced by the ayatollah Muhammad Sadr.

Then, too, coming from Islam, it was not certain that I could be accepted by the Christians from there, just as in Iraq, because my presence meant danger for them.

Since I had no intention of abandoning my fondest desire—to be baptized—I really had no choice: I had to take steps to leave as soon as possible—even though I anticipated that obtaining a visa would not be a simple matter.

Two days later something happened that confirmed my decision to leave the country. The owner of our house asked me to go with him to the office for residence permits, so that I could state my identity there. As we left the building, I was a bit uneasy about the procedure and begged him to explain to me the reason for it.

Thus I learned that in order to be able to rent to a foreigner, one must make a declaration to the government at the earliest opportunity. That allows the tenant to obtain a residence permit valid for three months from the department for foreigners at the Criminal Investigation Department [*Sûreté générale*].

On that same occasion the owner explained to me that when the residence permit expired, I would definitely have to leave the country or else pay a fine of a dinar and a half for every additional day spent on Jordanian soil. This meant that after three months I would risk being expelled from one day to the next, if I was arrested by the police.

I also realized with dread that the simple fact of stating my name and address at police headquarters would pose another great danger for me: that of being rediscovered someday by my family. Without knowing it, I had put the lives of my wife and children at risk. In a few minutes my decision was made: we had to move out as soon as possible.

Without any discussion, the devoted Sister Maryam moved heaven and earth. Within two weeks she had convinced friends of her religious community to take us in. They lived in a Christian village by the name of Fuheis, around twenty kilometers [12 miles] northwest of Amman.

The inhabitants of that small market town, located in the beautiful, verdant hills and valleys near the royal palaces, had the peculiar custom of never selling land to a Muslim, so that the families of Fuheis were exclusively Christian. It was an exception in Jordan, where the vast majority of the population is Muslim. Christians are more often in the minority, at the very most 4 percent. That is not negligible, but they are lost in the mass of five million inhabitants.

In Fuheis, on the contrary, Christianity makes itself visible: it is the only place in the country where the [church] bells ring and where the Way of the Cross takes place in the streets on Good Friday, in short, a haven of peace and safety for us in our daily lives—at least that is what we hoped.

We lived in an apartment located beneath the large house of our host family. The mother, Oum Farah, whom everybody in the village there called "Aunt", was a widow. She also had much to do, looking after her four children. Two of them wore the uniform, one in the army, the other in the police, whereas her daughters had devoted themselves to the Church. Having become financially independent, one of her sons vacated the downstairs apartment so as to build a house a little farther on, which allowed Oum Farah to welcome us into her home.

But for me it was difficult to accept that situation of dependency, which I found terribly humiliating. From the start I agreed only on the condition that I would pay rent. However, I quickly realized that for our host family it was not a question of running a hotel to earn money.

So I offered to contribute toward paying the electric bill. I was not sure that they would take me up on it, but at least it eased my conscience.

Very quickly I felt quite at home in that warmhearted family, where I was treated like a son. I was so at ease—too much so, perhaps—that I sometimes forgot my manners and the deference due to our hosts.

One day one of the sons of the household refused to go to a burial, pointing out that those people had not come to the funeral of his father. Yet that is a very important social duty in that country, as it is in Iraq also. Since I was present at the conversation, I slipped in a malicious comment: "An eye for an eye, is that Christian?"

As the days passed, these little details of our life made me realize that my presence was disturbing their very communitarian concept of religion. They did not hold it against me, for we were also developing ties of friendship and faith, but I sensed that they had been questioning themselves since my arrival.

With our history, we detonated in the middle of that very close-knit village community that was a bit withdrawn into itself. They were all Christians and were very much on the defensive in their relations with Islam. Their behavior was perfectly understandable when you know how much their daily life was troubled by all sorts of annoyances and aggressions from the Muslims.

One evening Oum Farah told me that at the university they once asked the Christians to stand up in the auditorium. Two or three young women had the courage to do so. They reaped copious insults from the rest of the students, first because they were not wearing veils, and then because they were not Muslims!

As a convert, I was a sort of extraterrestrial to the inhabitants of Fuheis. For them, going over from Islam to Christianity was absolutely unthinkable. [It was m]adness that is furthermore extremely dangerous. The very idea of conversion is totally foreign to them.

Given those circumstances, I was particularly touched by Oum Farah. She listened with emotion to our testimony and admitted to me several times that we had "reinvigorated" her faith since our arrival in her home.

For my part, I savored the good fortune of being able to live in the daylight with Christians. It consoled me after the trials that we had been through. I discovered also the pleasure of attending Mass every day, with complete freedom. That seemed to me to be an extraordinary blessing! Our stay in that village was so reassuring, with regard to both our safety and our faith, that within a month I was planning to settle down there for a while—especially since we had not made an inch of progress with our request for visas, if I was to believe the regular reports from Sister Maryam.

Besides, I listened to her with only one ear. I was much more preoccupied, on the other hand, with being baptized. And from that perspective, it may have been fortunate that our situation had become more stable. It is too good an opportunity to miss, I said one day to Anwar as we came back from Mass: let us try a new request.

I confided in Oum Farah, who was as kind to me as a second mother. I got the impression that the trials connected with my conversion and her own suffering as a widow quickly brought us closer together. Right away she had the idea of sending a message through her daughter Sana, a nun, who was well acquainted with Bishop Bassam Rabah. Together, we decided to write him a letter.

Alarm

Fuheis, May 2000

One morning I went to the market to buy a chicken for my family. Suddenly I saw Sister Maryam running after me, panic-stricken. When she had caught up, she was quite pale, despite the exertion. I sensed that something bad had happened.

"You must leave immediately; they have found you."

"Wait a minute. What about my chicken? Besides, who are 'they'?"

"Your sister Zahra. She surely did not come here alone.[1] Drop the chicken; you have to leave town right away!" she insisted.

Oddly, I did not get the same impression at all as Sister Maryam did that there was any danger—because Zahra loved me very much. I was sure that she had come with her husband to try to bring about a reconciliation. A priori that was no threat to our safety.

But the nun's insistent and anxious tone of voice prompted me to obey her; I walked back to our apartment. Along the way Sister Maryam told me that she had stopped by the house first. Unlike me, my wife had been completely panic-stricken by the news and had begun to scream.

I quickened my pace, worried about the state in which I was going to find my family, especially Anwar. Since our exile from Iraq, our wandering from one hiding place to the next, she had been living in a state of permanent anxiety and tension. I was afraid that this most recent incident would only make matters worse.

---

[1] A (Muslim) woman never travels alone; *marham* forbids it. This is a system that requires a woman to be accompanied by her husband, her son, her brother, or her father if she is to go anywhere.

No sooner had I stepped through the door of our apartment than my wife ran over to me and threw herself into my arms. The children were terrified by the agitation and were clinging to her skirts.

Concerned that she might attract the attention of passersby, I led them inside, followed by Sister Maryam. Once the sobbing had calmed down, the nun was the one who told me the particulars of the story.

"Sayid called me this morning," she began, "to tell me in detail about your sister's visit. She is looking for you."

"How did she find me?"

"She must have gone to the police, the department for foreigners where you had given your name. Through them she found your old landlord, who gave him Sayid's address", the nun answered. "Listen to what happened then; it's incredible!"

We sat down while Sister Maryam began her story.

"Just before noon three days ago, your sister rang the doorbell and Sayid's wife, Nawal, answered. '*Salam Aleikum*. I am Zahra Fadela al-Musawi, and I am looking for my brother Muhammad', she told her icily. 'My husband is not here.' 'May I come in and wait for him?' Zahra asked her. Sayid's wife was terrified, but she let her into her house so as not to break the sacrosanct law of hospitality. She was frightened even more because that morning her son Rami had been crying buckets, asking for his best friend Azhar."

As I listened to Sister Maryam, I remembered that during the two weeks that we had spent in Amman the two boys had become fast friends: they were the same age, seven years old, and got along wonderfully with each other, so much so that they spent twenty-four hours a day together! Azhar asked us almost every day to stay overnight at Rami's house. And when we left the city, their good-byes were heart wrenching.

"At that crucial moment," Sister Maryam continued, "Rami's mother was very much afraid that her son would betray them and talk about his friend. But it was too late to retreat; the enemy was in the public square. So your older sister sat down on the sofa, explaining that she had been sent by her father to settle a family conflict. Right beside her, young Rami was playing innocently, unaware of the drama that was unfolding. During that time, in the kitchen, his mother was preparing coffee for her guest, anxious that her son might open his mouth to complain once more about the absence of his friend Azhar. But Nawal was so paralyzed by fear that she no longer had the strength to call him so that he could go play elsewhere. The inevitable happened. Your sister insidiously questioned the child about his friends: With whom did he usually play? She asked whether he knew a boy of his age, Azhar. That was when the most extraordinary thing occurred. The same fellow who, a moment before, had been tearfully bewailing the loss of his friend, now declared that no, he did not know him, whereas no one had told him anything about Azhar's family. Do you realize how completely improbable that was? I think that it was a miracle", the nun said pointedly.

I was silently reflecting on the other child, mine, who in other circumstances had not been equally prudent. The disastrous consequences were such that I still shivered with dread at the thought of them. The ways of Providence in dealing with me were most certainly very mysterious: why yesterday, and not today? Maybe Rami had sensed from my sister's tone of voice that her question was not well-meaning, that she intended to do harm.

"Listen to what happened next", Sister Maryam continued. "Your sister was not discouraged for all that. When Sayid returned at noon she started to question him in turn. She asked him whether he had met the Musawi family in

Jordan. Sayid answered, 'An Iraqi did come to see me; he was asking directions to a house in the neighborhood. But I did not see him again, and I do not know where he went.' But your sister Zahra was not duped; she must have sensed that he was trying to pull the wool over her eyes; she offered five thousand dollars for Sayid to tell her the new address!"

I was stunned by what I had just heard. If my father was ready to spend an amount like that, it was because he was ready to go very far, to the worst extremes, to find me again and to make me return to Iraq. That did not reassure me in the least. At the same time, I knew my sister; she was the most intelligent one in the family: she could have tried her luck without actually having the money in her bag.

On the other hand, I was filled with admiration for Sayid, who had refused the offer. Here in Jordan he lived in poverty, doing odd jobs. All of his savings were gone, and he could have made use of that money to get his visa for Canada—not to mention the fact that we had not known one another for very long. Despite all that, he had said nothing, and I mentally expressed to him my infinite gratitude.

"You should know that your sister came back two days later to Sayid's house to try again. 'The owner of the house told me that you had been with the Musawi family at the time of their departure', she told him in a suspicious tone of voice. According to Sayid, it was heavy with implied threats, but he held out. When he told me the whole story," Sister Maryam concluded, "I slipped away immediately to meet you here. He did not dare to come with me, for fear of being followed. He will come later with his family."

I certainly had dear friends along my journey into exile. But that was not enough. I had to make a delicate decision:

to leave this protected place or not. Were we really safe in this village? That was the whole question. If they had tracked me down as far as Amman, no doubt they could find me here in Fuheis.

What reassured me despite everything was the fact that in order to learn about this place they would have to infiltrate Christian circles. That was much more difficult for them, being Muslims, than to get information at police headquarters—unless we were victims of a denunciation, but even then that information would have to reach them somehow.

And then the Iraqi dinar had been greatly devalued; I figured that their stay here was extremely costly for them: the hotel, food, travel. I was convinced therefore that they would not stay long in Jordan, even if my father did take care of all the expenses. This was quite likely, anyway.

Therefore, unless there was a new lead, my sister and her husband would probably return to Iraq, if they had not already done so. Three days had already passed. The alarm had been serious, but perhaps the crisis was behind us. In any case it seemed reasonable to me to make that wager, especially, I admit, since the prospect of a new exile seemed out of reach today. That would demand considerable energy, and I felt that I did not have the strength. I had not yet recovered from our stressful departure from Iraq. It was better to keep resting in this comfortable, welcoming house. Then I would plan for the future.

If we decided to stay a month or two, we would still have to take additional precautions. Despite everything, there was a risk that someone in my family might come back to Jordan to investigate.

We agreed with Sister Maryam that it was preferable for us to go out as little as possible, even to do errands. Oum Farah graciously offered to take care of them.

No more visits either, for the moment, from our only friends, Sayid and his family. So there we were, reduced to pacing in circles in the apartment, like caged lions.

Above all, I was afraid that this confinement would upset the equilibrium in our family yet a little more, especially that of my wife, whose psychological state worried me more and more. Since my sister had discovered our tracks, Anwar's nerves were raw and flared up at the least annoyance. She no longer slept; she cried all the time; she forgot everything, lost everything, and seemed incapable of concentrating on her work.

I felt quite at a loss; what could I do about her suffering? I did not know whether I should leave her alone, which she no longer could bear, or, on the contrary, be extremely attentive, but without irritating her even more. Fortunately, the presence of Monsignor Rabah or the nuns was able to calm and reassure her. That greatly helped me to be patient with her.

Anwar's nervous condition had its effect on our children, particularly our son, who sensed very strongly his mother's anxiety. At eight years of age, he was old enough to understand many things—in particular that he had been the factor that precipitated this situation by innocently making the sign of the cross in front of his grandfather. The responsibility was unbearable for the poor child. It gave him nightmares that I was powerless to dispel.

At the same time, Azhar did not understand that other people had changed his life. Formerly in Iraq he was the pampered grandson, the darling of his grandfather—and what a powerful grandfather, ruling over a clan and a considerable domain. As a result of that affection, everything seemed to belong to him: big houses, space, abundance. Everything was at his command, his slightest wish was satisfied the moment he expressed it, and his whims were respected.

From now on, there he was, the former prince, uprooted from that earthly paradise and living far from his family, from his grandfather, in a precarious situation with his anxious parents. How many times had he asked me why we had left, why we had made that choice? And I, his father, had not been able to find the words to explain it to him.

I was unhappy to note finally that we were as though in prison, condemned to remain shut in all day, although the bars were gilded. That awakened in me other more painful memories. I strongly sensed that the situation could not continue for long.

Baptism

Fuheis, June–July 2000

In our voluntary seclusion, the only time that we allowed ourselves to go leave the house was to go to Mass in the nearby church. We went as a family almost every day at seven o'clock in the morning and on Sunday for High Mass at ten o'clock.

I found in it great comfort, which helped me to endure the uncertainty in which we found ourselves. But I also sensed a growing frustration at not being able to receive Communion. And so I was champing at the bit while waiting for Monsignor Rabah's response to my request for baptism.

Unfortunately it was slow in coming, and every day that passed without news increased my impatience and made it painful. Waiting for the mail was thus the focal point of my day. But the lack of a response became cruel as day followed day; it was humiliating, inasmuch as it cast doubt on the legitimacy of my course of action.

It finally arrived at the end of June, the long-awaited letter. I was afraid to open it for fear of being terribly disappointed once more. My quick reading of it confirmed my fears. Its lapidary contents took away almost all of my assurance of being understood by the Church in that country. My letter was, it seemed, poorly formulated, and Monsignor Rabah asked me to write another one.

I was dumbstruck; the polished yet awkward answer made me feel once more that they were closing the doors of the Church against me. It was enough to make me despair of ever being accepted as part of the Christian community in that region. Would I have to wait again, to flee farther and farther, to Europe, in order to be entitled to baptism?

When I got over my anger, mixed with sadness, I tried to reason with myself: by acting in this way, Monsignor Rabah was probably trying to gain some time. He was telling me to keep practicing patience. As I read his letter more slowly, I finally glimpsed a timid overture on the part of the institution. It was up to me to seize my opportunity to storm the barrier, even though I did not see specifically how I could formulate my request any differently.

A few days later, in early July, before I had managed to find the solution, I attended the baptism of an infant, at which Monsignor Rabah presided.

During the ceremony I was revolted: he refused to give me what he was granting to a newborn! I was seething and wanted to go tell him off, and I no longer even heard the words of the liturgy. I rehearsed in my mind the arguments, the stages of my story that I wanted to explain to him so as to be understood. Because they had no outlet, my thoughts raced, collided with one another, and replayed in an endless loop.

The big scare that we had a few weeks before suddenly came to my mind. Fortunately the danger then had in fact passed. But if it were to happen again, and if this time it ended tragically, for me or for my family, I could not bear the thought of dying without having been baptized, especially when we were so close to our goal.

The end of the baptism ceremony arrived. I saw the cleric disappear into the sacristy. It was now or never. I then turned to Oum Farah and her daughter Sana, begging them to introduce me to him. I was determined not to pass up this opportunity that was being presented to me, perhaps the last one.

Since they agreed, I jumped up from my seat and dragged them by the arm, almost running, after the prelate. He seemed to remember my letter but did not appear troubled in the least. I took a deep breath and told him all at once, "You didn't require a letter from that newborn in order to baptize him! Well, I am a newborn in the faith."

I had been practicing mentally during the whole ceremony. I had repeated each one of the ideas that I wanted to express, the way in which I should present it, everything except that impulsive, abrupt sentence that came to my lips almost in spite of myself, from the depths of my battered heart. I was sickened.

But the man looked attentively at me, as though he were weighing each one of my words. He did not appear to be shocked by my remark but reflected a few moments before answering, "I must not have made myself clear. What I would like is for you to be able to prepare properly for baptism. I suggest a meeting sometime soon to explain it all in detail."

The following weeks were among the most beautiful of my life. From our very first meeting I was moved by the simplicity of the man, Bassam Rabah. Right at the outset he declared that he had been struck by my expression of being an "infant" in the faith, as well as by my perseverance.

Of course, I had two serious character references: Abouna Gabriel and Sister Maryam, two persons of note in the Christian community in Jordan and in Iraq. Monsignor Rabah knew them. Through them he was acquainted with my story; he knew also that he could have complete confidence in them. If they had taken care of me, they certainly had good reasons. For him, therefore, this matter was to be taken seriously.

During our four evening meetings in the month of July, I came to realize that this ecclesiastic radiated something profoundly human and considerate. He had a rare sort of kindness that was evident in his concern about little details to set us at ease, to overcome the distance between him and his interlocutors caused by his black cassock and his large pectoral cross.

When he spoke to us about baptism, I did not learn much that was new; Abouna Gabriel had prepared us well on the level of faith and Church teachings. But they were nevertheless impressive, beautiful spiritual meetings.

In simple words he explained to us the symbolism of the water used in the sacrament. Since I was acquainted with the desert, it was easy to understand that water means life. But, the pastor continued, water is also what cleanses from sin and makes possible a new life with Christ.

More surprisingly, during the next-to-last session Monsignor Bassam Rabah talked with us about the martyrs, those who had received the baptism of blood. They died for their faith and are now in heaven, enjoying eternal life.

That struck me deeply, since for years I had thought every day that it was quite possible that I might die for Christ—so much so that I was sometimes saddened by the idea that I could die an ordinary, natural death.

Thus, in the presence of Monsignor Rabah, I felt that I was being guided and trained in the spiritual life by a true pastor, like the "good shepherd" in the Gospel (Jn 10:11). I no longer had the sense that I was dealing with a haughty, inaccessible prelate who stood on ceremony.

At the end of those four meetings, no doubt judging that we were ready, Monsignor Rabah said something to me that calmed much of the anguish connected with the trials that I had been through: "You are knocking at the door of the Church, and the only thing I can do is open it for you."

With those few words, for the first time since our marriage and Anwar's conversion, we finally felt that we were truly in the Church, welcomed as full members and no longer as strangers who were tolerated but regarded with suspicion. That is how I had felt in Iraq, where our presence upset others.

My fondest dream was now to remain here, in Jordan, close to that man of God. For two months the situation had indeed cleared up a lot: my sister Zahra had not reappeared, and Monsignor Rabah, attentive to our needs, was thinking of hiring me for a job. I believe that the reason why he agreed to baptize us was because he hoped that we could be able to settle down in the region for a time.

Unfortunately that fine plan, I knew, was not viable in the long term. While we were still at the former house [in Amman], I had obtained a residence permit valid for three months, because I had been able to give an address. After our move to Fuheis, I had not reported a new address, out of prudence. The episode of my sister's arrival convinced me that I had followed a good inspiration.

But because of that, I found myself in an irregular situation. It was not very comfortable, and there was a risk of being sent back to Iraq at the slightest brush with the police, at the most insignificant difficulty that required me to state my identity. Our horizon was therefore restricted by the threat hanging over us. Although I was not happy about it, I knew that I would have to flee again someday.

That was why we had to arrange for the baptism to remain secret and to take place discreetly, so as not to risk provoking a reaction from the Muslim society, which was certainly less violent than in Iraq but no more open to religious freedom.

The other consequence was that I did not ask for a baptismal certificate from Monsignor Rabah. If there were a turn for the worse and I were sent back to Iraq, no one would know that I had officially become a Christian.

On July 22, just after noon, we went as a family, with the children, to a large church belonging to a religious community in the heart of the Christian quarter of Amman. It was a rather residential district, apart from the city life, although it was inhabited by Jordanians and not by expatriates.

Monsignor Rabah chose that church for reasons of safety, because it was part of a larger building complex, with multiple entrances. Therefore one could enter it more discreetly than a neighborhood parish church.

That day, inside that concrete building, there were not many of us sitting on the wooden benches, and the church seemed quite empty. There was the priest who was going to celebrate the baptism, another priest in a cassock who was assigned to be our godfather, and the godmother, a consecrated laywoman who worked for the monsignor. All of them had been carefully selected by Monsignor Rabah as trustworthy persons who were capable of keeping the secret.

Also present were a nun and the family that was hosting us, represented by Oum Farah. Not counting our two children, who were also to be baptized, there were nine of us in all. Monsignor Rabah had advised us against being baptized in Fuheis: friends and relations would surely have known about it. One day or another, the news would reach Muslim ears.

My only regret was that neither Monsignor Rabah, as a precaution, nor Sister Maryam, for other reasons, was able to come. When the date was set, the nun was in Iraq. When I contacted her to inform her about it, she asked me to postpone the day of the baptism so that she could attend.

But after such a long and painful wait, I had neither the patience nor the courage to put off the long-awaited ceremony again. If I postponed it, I told myself, Monsignor Rabah might very well change his mind and cancel the baptism. Having learned from experience the extreme prudence of the Church, which was inspired no doubt by the promises of eternity that she looked forward to, I was not ready to take that risk.

So there we were, all four of us, dressed in white robes that a nun had kindly made for us. Our hearts burning, we waited for the ceremony to start.

The long-awaited event, however, was tarnished a bit by the hostility toward Christians in that country. Indeed, mistrust had led us to take considerable precautions so that the baptisms would take place in the utmost secrecy. We knew that it was immensely dangerous to convert from Islam to Christianity in a Muslim territory. That is why, together with Monsignor Rabah and Sister Maryam, we decided not to celebrate all the baptisms at the same time.

In keeping with that plan, it was the children's turn first, while Anwar and I left the church. That way there was no danger that Azhar, who was about to become Paul, and Miamy, Thérèse, who was going on three years of age, would ever be tempted to denounce us someday, even by accident. I felt great pride in having somehow accomplished my duty by bringing my children, the flesh of my flesh, to Christ. Anwar and I had taken very special care to prepare them ourselves for this important moment.

Once the children had left to play outside, it was then our turn to receive the precious sacrament. With my head tilted forward to receive the holy water poured by the priest, I heard the solemn words pronounced by the celebrant: "I baptize you in the name of the Father and of the Son and of the Holy Spirit." And I thought of all those years of waiting and suffering during which I had sometimes believed that my final hour had arrived, years in which I never had any other aspiration than to live long enough to experience this moment.

At that second I was overwhelmed by a flood of mixed emotions.

Of course there was joy, the joy of that rebirth that Monsignor Rabah had spoken to us about, which signifies victory over evil. To me that was not a word that rang hollow, but, on the contrary, something very concrete, the scars from which I bore in my flesh. And to symbolize clearly that passage, that newness, I had chosen as my baptismal name the name of the evangelist through whom I had discovered Christ: John. As for Anwar, she had chosen to be called Marie.

But alongside of that still-fragile happiness there was fear. Despite everything, we could not set aside the thought that a climate of terror was weighing upon our little ceremony, if only by its clandestine character—not to mention that there was no going back on this commitment, which could mean persecutions for us in the future.

And then finally I felt a certain sadness in knowing that my own family could not be part of my happiness on that day.

After two hours of ceremonies, we gathered again, parents, children, and friends, in a little adjoining room to share a light meal. The priest who celebrated the baptisms had planned the thoughtful gesture. I thanked him from the bottom of my heart. As we lifted our glasses, we celebrated our entrance into the family of Christians. The warmth of those who surrounded us comforted me in the absence of my biological family.

It is true that there was a festive atmosphere in our little gathering, despite its stark simplicity. The children were delighted; they received presents from Sister Maryam and Sayid that were brought by the other nun. Everybody congratulated us, one after the other. I was surprised to hear the priest who baptized us say that it had strengthened his own faith. Even my godfather, who was also a priest, declared that he would never have agreed to baptize me; according to him, I had a faith greater than his!

He, however, was the one who said the Mass several hours later, and from his hands I received and ate with emotion, for the first time, "the Bread of Life".

A new phase of my life began for me that day, now that I could finally respond to the call of the man who had summoned me once in a vision that I still remembered clearly thirteen years afterward.

This man whose goodness and radiance had attracted me so much, this Christ for whom I had felt a genuine passion from the beginning—I had cherished him every day since then. Even in the darkest hours, there had not been a single moment in which I was tempted to abandon him so as to return to the gold-plated life that I had led previously.

From now on I could share in his life, in the promise of eternity that he brought me as the Son of God. If I could, I wanted to be able to partake every day of that bread of angels, to draw strength and joy from it, even several times a day if the Church permitted it.

After the Mass I felt that I was filled with an unusual courage, like a warrior running to combat, as if baptism and Holy Communion had made a new man out of me. Forgetting my situation and the circumstances hostile to Christianity, I wanted to leap and bound to communicate to those around me the overflowing joy that dwelled within me.

At a more prosaic level, this strength gave me that evening the resolve that I needed to put out what I considered to be my last cigarette. I was quite proud of that exploit, considering that I had started smoking while very young.

That was not all. In my enthusiasm, I wanted to be married in a Christian ceremony also. Monsignor Rabah had already explained to me, however, that there was no reason to do that: we had already been married before our baptism. Therefore I did not need to marry in the Church, even though I had been married in another religion. I was not sure that I was completely convinced by that explanation. For the moment I was content with it—while waiting to find a more thorough cleric.

At the end of that precious day, exhausted by so many emotions, we set out as a family on the road to Fuheis, so as to shut ourselves up once more in our apartment. But this time it was in thanksgiving for all that we had received that day.

"Zeal for Your House Will Consume Me"

Fuheis, late July 2000

Several days after our baptism, I telephoned Monsignor Rabah to ask another favor of him: would he please help me to find a job so that I could stop pacing in circles in this apartment?

The next day he called me and offered to meet with me during the day on the construction site of a new church, within the city limits of Amman. It was being financed by a Jordanian businessman, a descendant of a leading Christian family, for whom building a church was a point of pride. It showed his importance in the community.

Monsignor Rabah had spoken with him about my situation. Apparently he would have a serious lead for me. Therefore we scheduled a meeting in the afternoon.

When we met, the businessman, who was also the foreman, shook my hand warmly and asked my name.

"My name is Youssef", I told him proudly.

I had already been using that common first name simply for the sake of convenience. In Fuheis, a Christian village, it was unthinkable that I should continue to call myself Muhammad, as in my official papers. And so I had chosen this name, at the advice of Sister Maryam. Indeed, many former Muslims bore that name, which had the advantage of being able to serve just as well among Christians as among Muslims. And I kept it after being baptized, because everybody knew me by the name of Youssef. I even wondered whether that might be the reason why my wife opted for the name of Marie.

"And what is your father's name?"

I answered with silence, for I was extremely embarrassed by this new question from the businessman. Naturally it was out of the question for me to give Musawi as my family name. Even here in Jordan it would arouse suspicions about my religious affiliation. It was, however, customary to ask the family name, which situated a person in the social hierarchy.

"You do not know your father's name?" the foreman insisted.

I reddened with embarrassment. Fortunately Monsignor Rabah came to my aid by saying with a smile, "His father's name is Bassam Rabah!"

This, in a sense, was not completely false, at least with regard to the faith. Interiorly I thanked and admired the prelate. Once again he had understood the situation and had chosen the option that was favorable to me.

Thanks to which, the deal was concluded with a handshake. The businessman told me to meet him on the construction site the following day. I knew nothing about the building trade, but I was to be in charge of supervising the laborers, making sure that everything went smoothly, and managing security.

For the time being it was even planned that we could live in the rectory. Therefore our future was assured for the coming months. I started to tell myself that finally we could perhaps find asylum in this land, provided that we settled the problem of our resident permits.

Although I was very happy to be able to contribute any way I could to the building of a church, on the construction site I was very disappointed to find that the laborers were all Muslims and did not like Christians.

When I tried to understand their deep antipathy, they told me curtly that the Gospel had been perverted.

"Give me an example", I retorted.

"When it is written in your Bible that you have to love your enemies . . ."

For them, this attitude that Christ calls for was totally incompatible with the Qur'an. It demonstrated that Christians are despicable weaklings. That pained me, yet I was obliged to admit that my former coreligionists had nothing but hatred for the Church: it is deeply ingrained in their minds.

Sometimes I even had the feeling that I was running into brick walls, which threw me into a rage, for instance, one day after the consecration of the Church of the Holy Spirit. A few minor jobs remained in the interior of the building, and a Muslim laborer was working on them. At one point the man expressed his intention of climbing onto the altar with his shoes on, so as to be able to hang a chandelier.

I earnestly tried to dissuade him: "Don't move; I will bring you a ladder. Or at least remove your shoes."

"No, it's not worth the trouble!"

"But it is! I beg you, don't climb on the altar; it's sacred!"

The laborer then began to climb onto the altar while grumbling something that sounded very much like an insult to the cross of the Christians.

In hearing that blasphemy, my blood boiled. I pulled him from behind, threw him onto the ground, and lost control of myself; I began to beat him unmercifully. Overwhelmed by my strength and my weight, the man put up only feeble resistance. He was content to protect his face with his arms.

Suddenly I heard a dry sound, like a crack, and he started howling. I stopped short, out of breath from the struggle, and worried also that I had gone too far.

The laborer was driven to the hospital by the foreman and returned a few hours later with a plaster cast: he had a broken arm. Standing somewhat apart from the other workers who had flocked to the site, I stared at the ground, very uneasy about looking the foreman in the eye. He had gone to a lot of trouble on my account, and I wondered whether it could make him some enemies. At the same time, I felt no remorse. For me it was unacceptable that anyone should insult so crudely the most sacred thing that there is in my religion; if I had to do it over again, I would not hesitate for a second.

The foreman took me by the arm, led me to one side, and told me drily, "You are an Iraqi, you have no papers, and you cannot afford slip-ups like this!"

"But I begged him."

"That does not justify your act of violence! You will have to explain yourself to Monsignor Rabah."

Deep down I knew that he was right: I had acted instinctively, without thinking. I ought to have remembered that in Islam, the faith in which I had been brought up, blaspheming other religions was a matter of course. Thus Muslims thought that Christians had falsified the Gospel, in particular, by substituting a double for Christ crucified on the cross (sura 4:156).

But now that I had gone over to the other side, I could not accept this lack of the respect that was due to Christianity, whereas within the Christian minority I had never heard the slightest expression of animosity toward Islam, despite the fear, the harassment, and sometimes even the persecutions. This total lack of reciprocity between the two communities troubled me, and it was very difficult for me to accept it.

This is what I explained to Monsignor Rabah, who had been alerted by the furious foreman yet wanted nevertheless to hear my version of the facts. Facing the prelate I was in a tight corner, but I felt confident enough with him that I did not conceal what was on my mind.

Although he appeared pensive, I had the impression that my sincere words resonated with him. Bottom line: he must share my feeling about the great injustice endured by the Christians of that country.

After a few moments of silence, during which I anxiously awaited Monsignor Rabah's verdict, he was content with a few words, which he pronounced after a sigh: "You ought to have kept your cool."

"But it was impossible! I could have put up with it if it had been only about my family. But in this case the whole Church was being attacked!"

It is true that in just a few weeks (since the building project had begun quite a while earlier) I had invested myself enormously in this work, in this church under construction. For me it was not merely a question of an activity but much more than that: it was a concrete way of showing my attachment to the universal Church, my new family.

I had seen this religious building take shape and rise from the earth. I knew every nook and cranny of it by heart. When I reflected on it, what had happened that day with the laborer reminded me of the verse from Scripture when Jesus drove the merchants from the temple with a whip: "Zeal for your house will consume me" (Jn 2:15–17).

I was all the more attached to that brand-new church because even before it was dedicated we had obtained from Monsignor Rabah permission to live there with my whole family. That is what I wanted most in the world after my baptism: to live as close as possible to a church.

I kept the keys to it, like Saint Peter; I could open the chapel when I wanted. Indeed, that gave me a sense of profound responsibility: I was being useful and serving in the house of the Lord. For me it was also a sign of the love that I have for Christ, which had delivered me from the chains of Islam and had shown me the way of true happiness.

But today, because of my outburst, I was in danger of losing it all. I was perfectly aware of it. One word from Monsignor Rabah would be enough to send us back to our apartment in Fuheis, to our life of seclusion, like pariahs.

State of Grace

Very fortunately, I experienced once again how good and merciful a pastor Monsignor Rabah was, and how concerned [he was] about his sheep.

As my only punishment he took up my defense with my employer, asking him to settle the matter with the injured worker, so as to avoid a formal complaint by him. In no time at all a solution was found: the Muslim in question received a job offer at another work site that was even more enticing and lucrative, along with a significant bakshish [tip] to lull his conscience completely.

As for me, I tried to show the utmost gratitude by performing even more zealously my new duties as sacristan, which the clergyman had entrusted to me after the construction was completed.

Since the church quickly became a very busy place, I scrupulously made sure that the premises, including the rectory, were always meticulously clean. I even brought the children, who came with me when it was time to start cleaning at the end of the day. I was really pleased to see that they played the game [cleaning] spiritedly, won over, no doubt, by their father's enthusiasm.

Being sacristan allowed me to spend a lot of time with them in the chapel. Paul had benefited from our experience of the liturgy in Iraq, and he was already more advanced, but Thérèse had learned here, in just a few months, to recite the Our Father, then the Hail Mary, and even some chants from the Mass as she sat on my lap in front of the tabernacle. I still laugh about the time when she complained that her doll did not want to make the sign of the cross.

Anwar/Marie said that she had never seen me so happy during our marriage. Perhaps it was also because deep down I hid from myself the danger that my father had not yet given up his pursuit—no doubt so as not to have to think that someday we would have to flee again from the fragile security of our present situation.

In the very reassuring setting provided by the church and my job, and finally baptized, I had neither the courage nor the motivation to make new plans for a departure. And so I deliberately lent only a wary ear to the reports that Sister Maryam gave me about the steps in obtaining a visa.

Moreover, there was no lack of work for me in my job as sacristan. In the morning I accompanied the priest who housed us as he went to say Mass very early for a community of nuns in the Tlal al-Ali district. For the rest of the day I helped that priest in the church. He never failed to call on me on the slightest pretext, so that he gave me the flattering impression that I was indispensable. My days were long, quite filled with the many visits and the weddings for which I had to prepare the church and welcome the people.

During that time the children left for school each morning, all alone by bus. Monsignor Rabah had considerately set aside money from his own revenue so as to pay for their tuition.

For our whole family he was a sort of father, attentive to all our needs. That moved me tremendously. Several times he asked me to accompany him on his pastoral rounds. That enchanted me, for I greatly admired his understanding of the situations and the individuals that he encountered. The monsignor was able to get people to like him, especially the children, because he placed himself on their level when he spoke with them.

Overwhelmed by these precious experiences, I would have almost forgotten the hidden threat hanging over us, had it not been for the hostile environment in that district. Indeed, the inhabitants of the nearby houses, most of them Muslims, did not accept the presence of the new church so close to their homes. Their antipathy focused on the bells that rang every morning at six o'clock.

Several times this resulted in malicious acts, especially incidents of throwing stones at the church. By the end of the first month, the pastor of the parish therefore decided to silence the six o'clock bells, except for a major feast day or a wedding.

Despite the period of peace and the respite that we had enjoyed since our baptism, these little annoyances reminded me that prudence was necessary, and so I avoided going out too much, as Monsignor Rabah had advised me.

Therefore our friends, Sayid or the nuns, took turns visiting us instead. They also introduced us to other Christians, foreigners who spoke different languages but shared the same faith and the same hope. This sense of belonging now to the universal Church considerably softened our exile. So it was that we became acquainted with a charming, enthusiastic French couple, Thierry and Aline. He was a humanitarian aid worker, and she was of Lebanese descent, which made conversation easier.

On one of his visits, Sayid brought one of his friends, an Iraqi like us. I learned that he was originally from the mountains in the North, from a historically populated region in the foothills near Kurdistan,[2] where many Christians had always taken refuge down through the centuries.

As I asked him a few questions about his region, I was dumbfounded to discover that it was the same village

---

[2] Location of the biblical city of Nineveh.

described by Massoud, the first Christian whom I had ever met. When I pressed him to tell me news, he lowered his head. He announced that Massoud had been killed in an automobile accident only three days after the end of his military service.

Suddenly a whole phase of my story came back vividly, as if the years had erased the memory of it somewhat. For several moments I thought of the family that he had left on earth. I recalled also with emotion the blessed months that I had spent in the barracks with Massoud, when we recited the psalms together and made the most insane plans to flee my family. I saw myself again then, my soul exalted by accounts of the martyrdom of the first Christians. I listened to Massoud relate how they had not denied their faith during the persecutions, and I hoped to be animated one day by the same fortitude and courage. As for persecutions, I had not been spared them.

I also remembered the sorrow that I had felt at the time of the unexplained disappearance of Massoud. I had held a grudge against him for so long while I was running up against church doors and priests.

But now that I had finally found the explanation for that mystery, I was at peace. I finally allowed myself to look squarely at the slow progress that I had made, [during the] uninterrupted flight of thirteen years: my story, the long and painful quest that had left me uprooted, fatherless, someone living in secret.

When I was with Massoud I had had no difficulty imagining myself living in his village, a close-knit, homogeneous, reassuring Christian community, and starting a family there. That way I would not have experienced prison, torture, or the anguish of exile. Instead of that, I had to leave my family and my country. I had no choice; I had to go on.

But in doing so I had also been led to exceptional Christians, such as Abouna Gabriel, Sister Maryam, and Monsignor Rabah. Thanks to them, I ended up finding the door to the Church along my way.

From the first day, I had incessantly thirsted with an unquenchable thirst to be in communion with the man-God. He had revealed himself to me one night in a vision that had transformed my life. And because that communion brought me an unspeakable joy and fulfilled my heart beyond all imagining, I dared to hope that from now on I could feel at home wherever the Church is present, despite of the distance.

That did not do away with the suffering or the separations—Massoud, the break with my father, my land. Who knew what I would have yet to suffer? The future was still quite uncertain and threatening. Despite all that, I now believed that everything that had happened was part of God's plan for me. In learning so late about the death of Massoud, I understood that it could not be otherwise. I could not have hoped to live a more tranquil life.

Reconciled with my own history, I now felt capable of taking the next step confidently, abandoning myself to that will of God which is so impenetrable but, oh, how loving.

From now on I was even ready to confront the prospect of leaving this country where I had so many good friends. Since my arrival in Jordan, I had not dared to return to the French embassy to request a visa, as Abouna Gabriel had advised me.

On her own initiative, Sister Maryam had taken up the matter three months later, by meeting three times, thanks to her connections, with the French consul, Catherine du Noroit. At the request of the latter, a representative from the UN High Commission for Refugees (HCR) made a special visit one day to the embassy offices to see me and to study my request.

His name was Sofiane, and he was a lawyer of Algerian descent. When he arrived, the consul and Sister Maryam left us to have a private conversation, so that I could tell him my story. From the start I was instinctively on the defensive. I knew that the man was a Muslim, and so it was difficult for me to picture myself explaining to him my conversion, the source of all the persecutions that had followed. I also remembered the stories that I had heard in prison, in which individuals had been arrested following a contact with the United Nations agencies.

And so when he asked me for photos and a written account of my flight from Iraq, I flatly refused: "That is impossible."

I gave no reason to explain my strange conduct, for I did not want to get into a discussion about Islam with him. I stubbornly would not budge from my position. This exasperated him: "But you are mad! You don't realize how lucky you are! There are thousands of Iraqis like you lined up outside for a simple interview like this. And I made a special trip to the embassy for you."

Sister Maryam, however, had explained to me earlier that the Amman unit of the HCR had been created especially for Iraqi refugees. It accepted thirty to forty families a day, and only 15 percent of the requests were accepted each year.

That is why refugees camped in the street, sometimes for three days in a row, in front of the headquarters of the NGO [nongovernmental organization], merely for the opportunity to explain in five minutes the tragedy of their whole life and the reasons for their flight, hoping to convince their interviewer.

The man facing me could not get over it. "Besides, I know your story!" he added in a hurt tone of voice.

"If you know it, then you don't need me to write it down for you."

When I left the embassy I related the scene to Sister Maryam; she had been astonished to see the HCR representative leave in haste without even taking the trouble to greet them, his face contracted with anger. After listening to me, the nun tried to reason with me: "You are exaggerating!" she chided me. "This Sofiane certainly had good intentions. All Muslims are not that bad."

"You are a nun and you believe that everyone is good. You will see; that Algerian will do nothing to help us. On the contrary, he will throw wrenches into the works."

It was true that Sofiane's nationality had done nothing to gain my confidence. Reflexively I had adopted toward him the attitude of arrogance tinged with disdain that the Arabs of the Gulf have for their brethren from the Maghreb.

I must acknowledge that I had underestimated the tenacity of the nun in this matter, thinking that she would stop the procedures with the HCR there and then. But Sister Maryam was at least as stubborn as I; since the husband refuses, she said to herself, let's go talk to the wife. Thus she succeeded in convincing not only my wife, Marie, but also Sofiane, who apparently recovered from his wrath, to meet each other. Most likely the Algerian, who was married to a French woman and was very well connected in the French-speaking circles of Amman, had not dared to displease anyone by appearing openly vengeful, even though his status conferred complete authority over us.

During her interview with the humanitarian representative, Marie had fewer scruples than I: she spoke to him about my conversion, about hers and that of her children, about the prison, without concealing anything that might offend the faith of a Muslim.

Several weeks after that meeting, we learned that the HCR agreed to grant visas to Marie and the children, but not for me! The reason for this was given by Sofiane himself during a reception with the French. He claimed to have gained access to reports that I had helped to destroy churches in northern Iraq while I was in the army and that during my military service I had even participated in gassing Kurds in the same region. Consequently, I was not trustworthy in his view; my conversion itself was suspect, since I myself had persecuted Christians before embracing their faith.

No doubt he knew what he was doing in using such arguments with Western contacts, who in his view were necessarily Christians. Sofiane was also quite certainly aware of the repercussions that Saddam Hussein's violence against the Kurds had in Europe. My participation in that atrocity therefore could only discredit me.

When Sister Maryam related to me the duplicity of that man, I was not glad that I had been right. First, because in spite of everything he had sowed doubt about my credibility, then because my wife had not yet responded to the offer from the HCR.

Above all I realized that the arguments put forward by Sofiane bore the hallmarks of his adherence to Islam, despite his insistence on calling himself a secularist. How could anyone call into question the sincerity of my conversion under the sole pretext that I had persecuted some Christians? That proved for me his complete ignorance of Christianity and its history, starting with Saint Paul, who was himself the great killer of the disciples of Christ.

One considerable difficulty remained. What course of action would Marie adopt? She had within her reach a visa to go to France with the children but without me. For her that meant without any doubt whatsoever the end of the persecutions, the hope for a more stable and less dangerous life in a Christian country. Maybe I could join up with her later, after I had found some way of crossing the border. There was of course a risk, which was not negligible, that we might never see each other again. It was difficult to foresee what the life of an Iraqi Christian refugee would be like, in Jordan of course, but even in France. Above all I did not want to influence her decision, for I could appreciate all the responsibility that it involved, particularly with regard to the children. She courageously told the HCR that she had left Iraq because of her husband's faith and the difficulty of living openly as a Christian in that country, where the followers of Christ risked death. It would therefore be absurd for her to depart by herself with the children, leaving her husband, the one mainly concerned in their exile for safety's sake.

For me that was the greatest sign of love that she had ever shown me, greater even than her conversion, which, after all, concerned only the sanctuary of her conscience. But today for me, and exclusively for me, she was taking the risk of confronting new dangers. And she was perfectly aware of the fact that there would be no lack of dangers when the time came to leave the country. My wife's decision also acted as a soothing balm on my honor, which had been pilloried by the calumnies of Sofiane.

Fratricide

Amman, December 22, 2000

Despite the approach of Christmas, our little Thérèse could not manage to overcome her peevishness. Again this year her brother, Paul, who had been born in December, received his birthday presents. But this time, to add to the pain of his little sister, an attentive friend, understanding our destitution, had given Paul some new clothing.

She resented all this as a great injustice. The passage of days did not diminish her sadness; touched, I resolved to go downtown to find a little present for her, a dress, which would make up for her brother's good fortune.

I knew that it was not very prudent: [we had received] the advice to go out as little as possible, to go shopping in the neighborhood rather than in center city, although it was cheaper there. But after all, it would soon be Christmas, and my paternal heart spoke louder than my reason; besides, I said to convince myself, I am making just one trip there and back.

It was early afternoon, and therefore I had a few hours ahead of me before resuming my work at the parish. I took the "shuttle", which consists of small cars that seat three in the back and travel exclusively from one point to another, connecting various districts with center city. I found a dress quickly, so as not to waste time, and then waited in line for a return shuttle.

That was when I heard my name being called by the passengers of a car; there were five persons inside whom I could not see clearly because of the dusty windshield. Out of curiosity I approached the vehicle—a fatal error. After all those years, I had still not learned to be more suspicious!

Through the window I recognized, with dread, four of my brothers and my uncle Karim, the youngest brother of my father. Before, when we used to live together, I had been at the height of my power; they all were afraid of me. Now I was no longer the same man; I had changed. I wanted so much to explain to them, to make them understand what I had become. To that day I had not succeeded in laying claim to my faith in the bosom of my own family. The first time, when I was brought before the ayatollah al-Sadr, I had denied my Christian faith.

But this time I felt that I had the strength and the courage to witness and to speak quite frankly to them about

Christ. For me it was very important to be able to inform them of my baptism, so that they in turn could announce it to the whole family and their acquaintances. How naïve!

They all got out of the car, except the driver. They formed a circle around me. Oddly, I was not afraid. If I had to fight, I was bigger than they were and brawnier, too. Of course I had lost my influence over them, but I still felt able to make them respect me, with my fists if necessary.

Of course I did not imagine for a second that they might have weapons. And so I was not really frightened when one of them pushed me toward the backseat of the car and ordered me to come with them. "We'll have a talk. Just make sure we don't have any scandal in a foreign country!"

Despite the brutal tone, I was sure of my strength. I saw in this encounter a good opportunity to explain myself to my family once and for all. I would finally be able to settle indirectly my accounts with my father, to tell him about my bitterness over everything that he had made me suffer, which I had harbored in my heart for all too long.

I got into the car. In about ten minutes we had left the crowds of Amman and were in a desert valley. The car slowed down and stopped on the shoulder. The tension was palpable. I began to wonder whether I had not made a mistake in agreeing to come with them. We were alone. If it turned into a brawl, I could not expect help from anybody in that remote place. But the dice were cast. We got out to have our talk.

For three hours each side tried to convince the other. They tried to persuade me of the necessity of returning to my father and the advantages that I would have; I tried to explain the firm basis for Christianity, which prevented me from going back to be the Muhammad of before. Despite the menace that I detected in their eyes and their attitudes, I was not displeased with the opportunity finally to witness to my faith openly, to speak to them about Christ. Whatever happened afterward, those words would perhaps not be wasted on them. So I had the impression that I was taking part in the collapse of Islam, even though I knew, from sad experience, that the weight of Islamic society is a powerful brake on conversion.

The news about my family that I had just gleaned over the course of our discussion provided another example of this. I learned that our flight had created a conflict between our two families, the Musawi and my in-laws. After a month the police retrieved the car that I had abandoned in a parking lot in Baghdad. By the license plate they traced it back to my father. He immediately understood that I had left the country, which threw him into an insane rage. My in-laws, for their part, had also reacted very badly. To them, our departure together could mean only one thing: their daughter had consented because she too had become a Christian. And they could not tolerate that. Their pain was then transformed into continual reproaches against the Musawi, whom they accused of not having looked after their daughter-in-law Anwar adequately. They blamed my father above all, because he was the one to whom they had entrusted their daughter. That day I could gauge for myself how little in that society affection for one's relations mattered when family honor was at stake.

Morally the cruelest blow for me that day was admitting that my uncle Karim was the first to pull his revolver and point it at me. I could tell that he was a nervous wreck, exhausted by his failure to persuade me. But how could he go to such extremes when I had protected him in the past?

I remembered again the sums of money that he had borrowed from the family cashbox kept by my father, without ever repaying them [the family]. Every male had the duty of making his annual contribution to it, but he could also draw from it if need arose. The rules set by my father for the debtors were very strict: when a payment was due, it could not be even one day late. And so I used all my diplomacy to defend Karim against my father's intransigence.

If my father had chosen him for this mission, it was because he was ready to do anything to bring me back—anything, even to use someone in whom he certainly had only limited confidence. That was not reassuring to me, because it also meant that my uncle had been authorized to make use of the weapon that he was pointing at me at that very moment. My father must have told him, "You will bring him back to me, dead or alive!"

What followed remains a mystery to me. How did it happen that the first bullet, shot by Karim, did not hit me? What was that interior female voice that told me to run away at top speed? And the other bullets that came afterward, the ones that came very close to grazing me as they whistled past my ears—did they really miss me?

Before sinking into unconsciousness, my final thoughts were surprise at the burning sensation of a single bullet, the one that had made me fall into the mud, in that deserted valley.

When I came to my senses I was at the entrance to a hospital. In a daze, I felt that people were pushing me toward a double door, and I heard someone murmur to me, "Here is the emergency room." My head was groggy, I felt a stabbing pain in my leg, and I had the impression that I was awaking from a bad dream, a long and painful nightmare. As we went into the hospital, I gradually gathered my wits, enough at any rate for violent images of the last hours to well up into consciousness. I had the distressing feeling that I was almost experiencing a second time the attempt on my life: I heard again in my head the deafening sound of the detonations.

Exhausted, I leaned against the wall while waiting for the doctor who was to examine me. During that time I made a brief inspection and was vexed to discover that I was a piteous sight: soaked from head to foot, muddy, and convinced that I had been riddled with bullets, although I did not yet feel the sting of them.

As I looked more closely, I noticed that my wet jacket was perforated at the empty space between the arm and the trunk. I turned pale. This showed that I had escaped death by a few centimeters at most! In my misfortune I still had the extraordinary luck that Karim had very poor aim and that he had missed me, despite his first shot at point-blank range. No doubt about it: I had been protected.

Another incredible thing: I was standing and still had in my hands the little bag containing my daughter's dress. It was full of mud, but I had not let go of it during my frantic dash or during the trip to the medical facility. I was quite incapable of saying by what miracle I had been collected unconscious at the side of the road.

When the doctor arrived and brought me into a little room where there was a gurney [wheeled stretcher], I was struck by his eyes, in which I could read a wordless but insistent question. Surely, [it was] my outfit. I felt obliged to admit the truth from the start, to dispel his mistrust: "I have a problem: someone shot at me."

"Did you call the police?"

There was a question that caught me completely unawares. In the panic of the past few hours, I had been concentrating on my state of physical health, not on the criminal character of the attack that had been aimed at me.

From the doctor's perspective, however, it would be logical for me to alert the police first, except that ... Suddenly an idea occurred to me: "Listen, I would like to know whether I am really wounded, and whether it is serious. What I'm asking you to do is to examine me and to tell me whether my life is in danger. If so, then call the police. If not, I will go and simply return home. I don't want any trouble!"

Even with a wound, I knew that I was in danger of being expelled if I had a confrontation with the authorities. In the eyes of Jordanian law, I was in an irregular situation. If they learned, moreover, that someone had shot at me because I was a convert, they would probably finish me off themselves, so as to carry out Islamic law!

After examining me, the doctor left me alone with my thoughts, stretched out on the metallic cot.

His absence revived my fears. Imagining the worst, I already saw myself handcuffed and thrown behind bars. Fortunately I was relieved to see the practitioner return, accompanied not by a policeman but by a nun. So from now on I was reassured and certain of being in good hands, those of the good Lord, or almost.

The nun in question was in charge of the hospital; she had been alerted immediately about this case, which was at least unusual in her institution. Facing her, I felt confident, [confident] enough at any rate to ask her whether she knew Sister Maryam, in that Christian community which had been reduced to a few tens of thousands of believers. And sure enough, Sister had just left the hospital, where she customarily visited the sick. No doubt we had even crossed paths. I was definitely lucky.

After they called her on her portable phone, the nun set out again right away for the hospital. While waiting for her, I asked the directress about the state of my health. The doctor assured her that the wound was not too serious. Only the calf had been hit. I breathed a sigh of relief. About twenty minutes later Sister Maryam burst into the room, out of breath from having walked quickly. They informed her in a few words about my medical situation, and she asked them to let me stay at the hospital to be treated there, just to be safe.

Oddly, the directress shook her head as a sign of refusal. Pressed by Sister Maryam to explain her decision, she admitted, with some embarrassment, that it was not possible to keep me.

"It is too dangerous for the hospital. It could be closed definitively if news ever got around. And then . . . Monsignor Rabah himself is ordering me to discharge this man."

Sister Maryam was furious. As for me, I felt no resentment, because I was very fond of Monsignor Rabah. I understood his reasons, the weight of his responsibilities, the prudence necessary so as not to endanger the whole community. And it was true that my life was not in danger, at least not from my bullet wound.

But I could not help feeling rejected once more, like someone with the plague, because I had committed the worst possible crime in the house of Islam: I had denied the Qur'an and chosen Christianity. Where was the justice in that? Would I have to flee for my whole life in order to expiate my sin?

Faced with those questions, I felt terribly alone. The directress lowered her eyes; she scarcely dared to look at me. No doubt she had some dim awareness of the severity of her decision, even though she did not know my story. But the nun had made a choice. I did not blame her for that. In her place, maybe I would have acted the same way.

Thank God there was Sister Maryam. As always, she kept her cool. I admired in her that practical intelligence that allowed her to maintain control of events even in the most perilous situations. She imperiously asked the directress to hail a taxi for me. Her idea was to send me off in it wrapped in a white sheet, so as to hide me from the eyes of the curious.

A wise precaution: indeed, it was quite possible that my brothers were still in the area, watching the comings and goings around the hospital. After all, I still did not know who had been the Good Samaritan who had picked me up from the side of the road. She had noticed him because he had driven off with the tires squealing, whereas usually it is the opposite: people arrive at top speed—someone else hurrying to go home after a day of fasting during Ramadan, the nun had thought.

It was also likely that my rescuer's haste had been due to the risk that he had taken by picking me up, wounded, without knowing whether I was a dangerous criminal. At the very least it would have meant suspicions and long explanations to the police. Or else, another possibility [was that] he had witnessed the whole scene of the attempt on my life and had fled right away after dropping me off at the hospital, for fear that my killers were following him.

Wrapped in my sheet on the backseat of the taxi, I was lost in conjectures about the identity of my benefactor, and even more about the mystery of my rescue in the middle of the desert. I might just as well have remained lying there, waiting for help while losing blood.

Another mystery: how did that unknown person manage, alone, to lift into his car a man weighing ninety-five kilos [209 pounds]? And how did it happen that my brothers had fled, without even making sure that I was really dead? Was it neglect, or panic about having gone too far and now having to explain it to my father? Or maybe they had been routed by the arrival of my benefactor. I would never have an answer to those questions, but I thanked heaven for protecting me, whoever had been instrumental in doing so.

At nightfall the taxi arrived at the church at the same time as Sister Maryam. She had time to warn my family, as well as three doctors, one of them a surgeon: all Christians and friends of the nun, so there was nothing to fear as to their discretion.

My wife was terrified. She was trembling at the thought of seeing my brothers reappear. Our children were clinging to her, uneasy about their mother's fear. I held her tight, without finding any words to reassure her.

I myself was at the end of my strength. I felt weary, physically and morally, drained by this battle against adversity. Besides the fear of dying, I was quite shocked at seeing my brothers shoot at me.

Perhaps that was even the most difficult thing to accept; I had the feeling that a cold, implacable violence had been unleashed against me. The fact that it came from my own family only added to the brutality of the act. It was a betrayal that affected me very deeply, in a spot where until then parental love had given me a firm foundation and confidence in life.

Even the ordeal in prison had not impaired that certitude, because I could tell that my father still had affection for me, despite everything. Life together with my clan had become unlivable for me, but with distance I had thought that we might once again understand and accept each other, despite our religious differences. Now I realized with immense sadness and a great bitterness that it was no use; our ties had been broken definitively.

A cry of pain tore me from my embrace with Marie. I suddenly felt the sting of my wound returning. I had to lie down if I did not want to collapse onto the ground.

At my bedside, one of the doctors explained after examining me that the bullet had indeed gone in, but without exiting; there was only one wound. He then showed me the place where that bullet must still be, since he could feel it under my skin.

The physician added that my delayed pain was quite consistent with a wound caused by a firearm. At first I had felt no pain because the temperature of the projectile was very high; only after the bullet cooled did the pain appear, like a sting.

More troublesome was the fact that the bullet was still in my calf. That meant that they had to make an incision to remove it, hence the need to have [a] surgical facility, and therefore a hospital. But where? The three colleagues, with Sister Maryam's help, took the trouble to telephone all the private clinics in the area, trying to find one that would accept me. Wasted effort! Not one was willing to take the risk of accepting someone with a bullet wound. It was too dangerous, because for them it implied the certainty of having to deal with the police.

During that time, stretched out on my bed, my leg up in the air, I listened to them discussing the best course of action to take in this perilous situation. If someone did not operate quickly, I was in danger of developing a bone infection; the wound was deep and certainly involved, in the opinion of the three doctors, a good dose of filth from the mud in which I had fallen. This implied, long term, the possibility of an amputation.

I was reduced to imagining that distressing prospect when, suddenly, I felt a hot liquid flowing along my leg, to the thigh. "Come here! I'm bleeding", I cried, distraught.

The three doctors hurried over and verified that there was indeed blood trickling, but from the other side of my calf, opposite the place where the bullet had entered. I did not understand what was happening to me. And I had the unpleasant impression that the physicians had no idea either.

As they looked at me, the three specialists seemed to go limp, baffled by this phenomenon that apparently was not part of their scientific repertoire.

I wanted to scream, partly from fear, partly to awaken them from their reveries. The surgeon got a grip on himself, however, and prepared to make a bandage for me. He took my leg and was starting to wrap it in white gauze, when he suddenly froze.

Once more he probed my calf: "The bullet . . ."

"Well?" the other two asked in chorus.

"It . . . it disappeared!"

And each of my three doctors palpated the leg in turn. Then they went over the whole room around the bed with a fine-tooth comb, without managing to turn up the projectile. The bullet could not be found!

Eventually I was amused by that little scene, which lasted a good half hour with no results. I even forgot the pain, which was dulled as a result of the spectacle that I had before my eyes.

Since they could not retrieve the bullet, one of the doctors finished the dressing. Out of professional conscientiousness and pride, he promised to find for me the next day a hospital that would agree to make some radiology tests, so that science could reassert its rights over against the unexplainable.

That same morning I found myself once again wrapped in a blanket and driven by Sister Maryam to a hospital. Surprise: the X-ray showed no signs of a lesion inside my leg.

With such a wound, the bone would certainly have been hit, and they would have had to amputate my lower leg. It seemed, though, that the bullet had followed a strange trajectory in my calf: neither the muscle nor the bone had been touched. This implied that the projectile had made several zigzags so as to enter by one wound and leave by the other.

One hour later, in the car on the return trip, the doctor who had insisted on driving me to the hospital, who was rather agnostic, confided to Sister Maryam that this was a red-letter day for him. Everything that he had seen since the previous day seriously shook his convictions as a rationalist physician. From now on he could just as well believe in the Resurrection of Christ!

Not being a physician, I had no trouble giving credence to the idea of a divine intervention on my behalf. After all, it would not be the first time, and you have to admit that one becomes accustomed to everything, even miracles.

What astonished me, on the other hand, was that I recovered so quickly from my wound. In less than a week the wound had disappeared and I felt almost no pain. So there I was, back on my feet, not counting the crutch that temporarily accompanied me on my walks.

From One Flight to Another

Karak, December 26, 2000

Four days after the attempt on my life, in the middle of the night, Sister Maryam hurriedly drove us to a little forsaken village in the South, in the region of Karak, three hours away from Amman.

I felt guilty. To some extent this was all my fault. The nun had strongly advised me not to leave our apartment. But I couldn't help doing so anyway, to help the parish priest.

He had health concerns, and without me he was lost in the new church, which I knew like the back of my hand, certainly much better than he. Even to turn off the electricity he could not do without me. And so despite my crutches, I answered his calls for help, at the risk of compromising our safety. When Sister Maryam came to visit us and found out, she flew into a rage: "You do not know what risks you are taking! If someone ever sees you, you are dead!"

That same evening, therefore, we had to wake up the children in the middle of the night and move the whole family, without even alerting the priest, who would no doubt be opposed to my departure. Braving the thunderbolts of our protectress, I had dared to mention the idea of saying goodbye to that good clergyman and telling him how happy I had been to look after his church. But I had not counted on the resolve and intransigence of Sister Maryam. Besides, I had yielded without arguing. Having learned from experience, I now knew that our safety depended on our discretion.

After hours on the road in pitch darkness, on a winding desert road with hairpin turns through hills and valleys, we finally arrived at a little parish. The inhabitants were tribes that had remained Christian in a predominantly Muslim environment. Sister Maryam visited them from time to time to teach catechism.

Always thinking ahead, the nun had gone shopping that afternoon so as to enable us to live independently for several days in a little house adjoining the village church. After making sure that we had settled in, she left us, promising to come back in two or three days with more provisions.

On her second visit one evening Sister Maryam surprised us by bringing with her Oum Farah. The widow from Fuheis had asked so insistently to see us that the nun had finally given in.

The evening went on until rather late; none of us dared to disrupt the fragile harmony of the party. It was such a

change from our monotonous seclusion. Marie and I knew
how precarious our situation was, and so we were happy to
find a bit of warmth in being with our friends.

Around ten o'clock someone pounded violently on the
door. A loud voice startled us all: "Police!" I was paralyzed,
incapable of the slightest reaction.

I would never have imagined that someone could find
me in that forsaken place. Even Maryam, usually a very
resourceful woman, seemed lost, suddenly dumbfounded by
this new turn of fate.

The policemen—there seemed to be at least two of
them—continued to knock on the door, at ever shorter
intervals that manifested their impatience.

Then, taking the initiative and summoning her courage,
Oum Farah got up and walked resolutely to the door. She
prudently opened it halfway. "What can I do for you?"

"We want to see the Iraqi who is here! To find out
whether his papers are in order."

"Come in, then", Oum Farah calmly replied, opening
wide the door to them.

"No", one of the two men answered firmly. "Our
mission is to bring him in to the police station for
interrogation."

"Gentlemen, please do come in and have a cup of coffee", the widow insisted, taking their arms and guiding them
inside, with the benevolent but imperious voice of the lady
of the house who does not compromise in observing the
laws of hospitality.

Aware that they had no choice, given so many kind attentions, the two policemen in civilian clothes sat down in the
little parlor facing me. Suddenly they seemed numb, less at
ease no doubt with polite company than with conducting
an interrogation. But their embarrassment did not last, and
they quickly resumed their role of investigators.

"What is the name of this man across from us, who strangely resembles the one we are looking for?" they asked Oum Farah.

"My name is Youssef", I answered, almost apologizing for speaking up.

I was in a tight corner: I was unable to say more than three words in a row coherently, and I had no idea how I was going to get out of this predicament. Fortunately Oum Farah once again came to my aid: "I suppose that you know Raad Balawi; he is also with the police, a rather high-ranking officer, I think. He is my son!"

For an instant, amazement came over the faces of the two policemen. They were dealing with someone who could cause them some trouble. While we were wide-eyed with astonishment, Oum Farah took advantage of the element of surprise so as to press her advantage and turn the tables of the interrogation.

"Can you tell me who it is exactly that you are looking for?" she said to them with a cajoling smile. "If I can help you, I will be glad to do so."

"We are looking for an Iraqi who has a wife and two children", said the older of the two men, regaining his self-control. "The man there with you fits the description. We want to know whether he is the one. Show us his passport."

The man spoke in the tone of someone who is used to being obeyed. He must be the chief. He did not seem to have been taken in by Oum Farah's show of friendliness, or at any rate it did not make him forget his duty.

Our protectress then tried one final dodge: "Unfortunately his passport is at the embassy. I promise that some-one will bring it to you tomorrow."

These last words of Oum Farah were spoken with much less assurance. It seemed more like a plea. I was afraid that now, having exhausted all our arguments, there was nothing left to do but to follow them. My future again appeared very bleak.

But the dreaded order did not come. Dumbfounded, I watched the two policemen stand up and take their leave while glancing at me suspiciously. They had not been convinced of my innocence, but at least they were going. I wanted to hug Oum Farah for her composure and for the way in which she managed to turn the situation around.

It is very likely that the widow's distinguished air, as well as her connections, had kept the policemen sufficiently at a distance that they did not dare to use their authority and bring me to the station by force.

During the decisive minutes of that battle of wits that had played out before our eyes between Oum Farah and the policemen, each of us passive observers had held his breath. Now at last Marie served us a glass [of wine] to calm our frayed nerves.

"How can it be," I said in astonishment, "that Oum Farah insisted on coming precisely this evening? Anyway, it's extraordinary! Without her I would not have stood up to the policemen for one second!"

"All the more reason," the widow remarked, "because they must have been from the secret service, since they were not in uniform." But that did not explain how they had found me so quickly. Here was another riddle besides the mystery of my brothers' presence in Amman.

I began to think that I was constantly under surveillance, invisibly, maybe by satellite. No doubt that was paranoia, but for me that was the only explanation for these troubling coincidences. If the secret service had tracked me down to this little village, then I was no longer safe anywhere.

As for Sister Maryam, she leaned toward another explanation: a quarrel between two neighbors in the preceding days must have degenerated, as often happens. I then had served as a scapegoat; it was easy to put the blame on a foreigner like me by reporting me to the authorities.

Whatever had happened, we were in danger. We had to flee again, but to where? Sister Maryam had no idea, nor did I. Oum Farah suggested returning to Fuheis, so as to gain time to find another solution.

The next day at four in the morning, Marie and I awakened the children and headed for Amman. We did not regret leaving that village where people looked at us distrustfully. Even the nun realized with regret that she could no longer come teach there; it had become too dangerous for her. From now on she would have to send other nuns.

So as to avoid the risk of being arrested, we did not take the same road back. Certainly that route was more direct, but also more heavily traveled and therefore liable to be under police surveillance.

We arrived in Fuheis in the early morning. Our plan was to leave again as soon as possible, taking just enough time to call Monsignor Rabah and beg him to find us a hiding place. No luck.

Four hours later we got back into the car, our children on our laps, to go to the north of the country this time, to Zarqa. The town was large enough for our presence there to go unnoticed. And Sister Maryam had contacts there among the missionaries who had a vocational-technical school and a parish in the vicinity.

Along the way the nun explained to me that this industrial town was quite well-known. There, in September 1970, three airplanes had been hijacked by Palestinian terrorists. From then on King Hussein decided to expel the Palestinian refugees from his country, in operation Black September.

After about twenty kilometers [12 miles], the car stopped in front of a student residence where, thanks to the nun, we had obtained permission to occupy part of the dormitory for one or two weeks during the school vacations.

Respite

Zarqa, February 2001

When the students returned, we moved to a spacious house made available by Monsignor Rabah, situated just outside the town. Upon arriving I was happily surprised to find, adjoining the building, a little chapel in the midst of a large plot of land that could be cultivated. We would probably stay there for several months, during which time Sister Maryam would go through the long administrative procedures involved in obtaining a visa for me.

I was now convinced of it: we had to go again into exile. Here or in Iraq, life would always be impossible for us Christian converts, inasmuch as the governments of those two countries would regard Sharia, Islamic law, as the sole source of law, and they would not allow the fundamental liberty of changing one's religion and abandoning Islam.

I hoped, without much conviction, that we would not be obliged to flee to the West, where the language would be a major obstacle to our integration. If I had had a choice, I would have preferred an Arab country where freedom of conscience is more readily accepted. I was thinking in particular about Lebanon, in which Christians even have an officially recognized place, or else Syria.

Whatever our final destination, leaving Jordan would certainly be another trial for us, a difficult obstacle to get past. In any case that is what a retired military man, Oum Farah's uncle, gave me to understand when I confided in him one day; according to him, there was a great risk that we would be arrested at the border.

For the moment I refused to be tormented by that threat, because I had other more immediate concerns. First I had to find a school for our little Paul, who could not be allowed to interrupt his studies, which had been haphazard because of our many travels.

Thanks to Monsignor Rabah, he was accepted at a little Christian school. Every morning a bus came to pick him up, and in the evening it brought him back. When he returned, I closed the doors and shutters and double-locked them, and thus we cloistered ourselves until the next morning, unless a visit was planned.

The strict rule that I had set for myself, at Sister Maryam's advice, was never to go out, except to go to Mass, and not to open the door to anyone, under any pretext, unless the arrival of friends had been scheduled in advance.

I was not reassured; maybe I never would be again. What guided me now was fear, fear that the police would find me, fear also of the Muslim district around the house. I was not sure that we were welcome in the neighborhood.

Sometimes, at the end of the day, we were startled to hear a dry tapping on the house, like a heavy hail. One evening, so as to get it off my mind, I went out and found to my dismay that it was pebbles that had been thrown from the road. But apparently no one claimed responsibility for that malevolence.

The inhabitants all around us must have noticed that the little cottage was full again, and they took advantage of the opportunity to show their hostility to Christianity, symbolized by the presence of the little chapel.

As for me, I was used to this violence on the part of Muslims, and personally I had experienced worse than a few thrown stones. But I trembled for my children, who were disturbed by it each time and sought refuge with Marie or me.

Despite the animosity from outside, we spent happy days and weeks there, in seclusion, but visited by our friends, Sister Maryam, Oum Farah, Monsignor Rabah, and Sayid and his family, for convivial meals.

The uncertainty of our future probably contributed a lot to that sentiment. We appreciated more intensely those blessed moments, which were like an oasis before going back to the desert of our life as exiles. In those moments of friendship there was a taste of eternity, paradoxically by the very fact of their fleeting character, and no doubt because of the time that we spent praying in the chapel as a family.

Thanks to the hymnal and the Gospel book, both of which we received from the hands of the pastor of Holy Spirit parish where we were living, we nourished our prayer with the Word of God and songs of praise.

Day after day I drew from the psalms, in particular, a serenity and a confidence that surprised even me, even though we were in a very uncomfortable situation. Instead I had within me, incomprehensibly, something like certainty that I would not be abandoned. So I managed to conceal completely the thought of our inevitable departure and preferred to concentrate on day-to-day life.

"What I miss most", I confided one evening to Sister Maryam, "is that I'm not working."

"Don't even mention working or going out; I already have high blood pressure!"

So I consoled myself by planting some vegetables on the plot surrounding the house, but that was not enough for me. I would still have to earn my living so as not to depend on the generosity of the nuns.

One fine day, in a fit of independence and pride, I refused the provisions brought by Sister Maryam.

"I paid for them with your money," the nun replied with a sigh, "with the two thousand dollars that you left with us for safekeeping."

I was not sure that that was true. But I secretly was worried, seeing my little stash melting like snow in the sun.

Farewell to the Near East

Zarqa, July 2001

During our exile far from Amman, Sister Maryam followed up on our application at the embassy. It was the only way left for us to obtain exit visas, after the failure of one attempt with the High Commission for Refugees. Secretly she conferred with her contacts, without reporting to me exactly what leads she was pursuing or the possible destination.

In late July she triumphantly announced to me that she had succeeded in obtaining visas for us, which would be delivered to us on the condition that we found a host family in France. She confided to me that the attempt on my life had greatly helped to convince the French authorities.

I had an appointment two days later at the French embassy with the consul, Catherine du Noroit, to pick up the precious documents and to finalize the details of our departure.

As we went to the interview, I did not dare ask Sister Maryam any questions. I was afraid that I would hear myself agreeing that we would have to flee to France. I did not know that country, but for me it meant one thing: leaving this region, my region, and the Arab world, to go to a land where I would be a foreigner, since I did not have a command of the language.

Sister Maryam explained to me anyway that our exile was imminent, at the latest one month away. The news caught at my throat; I was almost suffocating, so great was the gnawing anxiety at the thought of that sudden departure.

So with my stomach in knots, I walked with Sister Maryam into the embassy, through a hidden door at the back of the building. Despite this precaution, we passed in the corridors an Iraqi who stared at me for a long time and finally told me, "I know you!" I did not answer, pretending that I had not heard anything. But that unexpected interruption did not bode well at all for what was to come.

In the consul's office I remained a bit withdrawn, slightly intimidated. I let Sister Maryam handle things, as was usual for her. For a moment the two women spoke quietly. I did not understand a word of their consultation, but suddenly I saw the nun blanch. My jaw clenched.

"What is going on? Tell me the truth!"

The nun was the one who answered, with a helpless gesture: "There is a problem."

I kept quiet, anticipating a catastrophe and already resigned to the worst.

"Your names are posted at the borders."

"Which means?"

"Which means", Catherine du Noroit interjected, "that you are probably being sought by the Jordanian police and that even though France has granted you a visa, you would be taking a great risk in trying to board an airplane."

I was floored. First, the meeting confirmed that our final destination was France after all, which for me, frankly, was no cause for rejoicing. Furthermore there was very little chance that we would succeed in arriving at that goal, with invisible pursuers on our heels.

And even if we succeeded in crossing the border at the Amman airport, I imagined with dread that secret agents would pursue me wherever I went, in France as well as in Iraq or Jordan. I would never manage to escape my family's desire for vengeance. I already saw myself arrested and imprisoned in France, overtaken by that permanent threat that was weighing on me.

But Sister Maryam seemed to have recovered her usual cool demeanor and spoke energetically to the consul: "The French embassy must do something to get him out of this predicament! Issue an order to let him leave with his family."

I admit that I did not have much faith in it. From then on I was very pessimistic about our chances to extricate ourselves from this international manhunt alive.

Until then I had had faith in divine protection, but I had also been counting on my own strength, on my resistance to evil, to get through and to overcome the toughest trials. I had taken a certain pride in it, assured as I was of my lucky star. Having reached this stage where I no longer had any resources of my own, no concrete way of getting beyond that impasse, I had no choice but to abandon myself to the inexplicable designs of Providence.

From the human perspective, the situation seemed quite bleak. Perhaps I should even resign myself to the loss of my own life. I pictured myself dying gloriously as a martyr for the cause of God, and that prospect condemned me to wandering around like a poor beast that knows instinctively that someday it will fall into the hunter's snares.

The fact of having endured all those torments, only to end up as a miserable wretch, made me infinitely sad. I had no other recourse but my poor, almost wordless prayer; moreover, my thoughts were like a hopeless battle that I was waging against myself so as not to sink into destructive bitterness. My adversaries would then have gotten the better of me, without having to unsheathe another weapon. Islam and the society that proceeds from that religion would have deprived me of the most basic liberty. That freedom alone would have enabled me to live in peace in that territory in the Near East that also belongs to Christians.

Within a few days, Sister Maryam's stubbornness had gotten the better of my bout of fatalism. No doubt her faith had nine lives, being more firmly rooted, the deep faith that moves mountains—faith, and several well-situated connections. By dint of reexamining the question from all angles, the nun remembered that one of the sisters in her community taught catechism with the wife of a high-ranking official at the French embassy, Pierre Tivelier.

The next day his wife found herself in possession of the whole dossier containing all my proceedings, my story, and several photos—and, above all, a handwritten letter meant to convince her husband the diplomat to facilitate my departure from the country. From a woman's lips to God's ear!

The saying proved true a second time: a week later, Sister Maryam told me that two members of the Jordanian secret service would be present at the airport to protect me if things turned bad. The nun explained to me that this was special protection that I quite certainly owed to the embassy's intervention with the king himself. The day of departure was scheduled for August 15, in less than two weeks.

On the evening of the fourteenth, Monsignor Rabah personally came to bid us farewell. I was extremely moved by this kindness, for in a few months I had become attached to him as to a father. That evening especially, his company calmed me when I was feeling torn away from my land, like a leaf fallen from a tree to the ground, swept by the winds and trampled underfoot.

During these past sixteen months in Jordan, my meeting Monsignor Rabah was one of the greatest blessings that I had received, for his fatherly presence had made up for my emotional desert. In my family, in Iraq, I had been constantly overwhelmed with consideration and attentions. In the street, people greeted me by the title Sayid Maulana, that is, "our lord". If I rejected my baptism and decided to return to my family, I knew that I would have palaces, servants, and courtesans. But I wanted to live in an Iraq where Christians would have rights as citizens; I wanted society to change, or better, to become Christian. While waiting for that day, here I was, condemned to be a stranger, alone with my family, tossed about from one exile to the next. I believe that Monsignor Rabah sensed that emptiness in me, and that was why he had been attentive. I will never forget that one day he declared that he was my father.

I think also that the fact that we both belonged to the Near East brought us closer together. With Abouna Gabriel it had been different. I [we] had had a more distant relationship, that of teacher and disciple. The European friar had taught Marie and me and rooted us in the faith, but the signs of affection had not been as strong. It still pains me that he did not try to find out news about us after our departure from Iraq.

On the eve of our departure, I thought again also of that Gospel passage that Abouna Gabriel had quoted to us: we must be able to leave everything for Christ, and it would be returned to us a hundredfold, somewhat as Abraham, our distant Iraqi ancestor, had done.

I left a lot of myself behind in leaving the Near East, particularly those two pastors who had taught me everything.

I would have liked that evening to last forever, so as to keep experiencing the almost childlike joy of contact with that clergyman who was so simple and so filled with God. As was his custom, he did not eat much—some broth and a little water. That evening I realized that that was no doubt the secret, the key to the goodness that emanated from him. Because he was an ascetic, no longer controlled by his body and its appetites, he left all the space inside him to Christ and made him radiate around him.

As he was about to leave, after Monsignor Rabah had already given us almost four hours of his precious time, the sadness that I felt at the thought of our separation was not unbearable, as if I sensed that we would see each other again. Proving his great sensitivity, Monsignor Rabah also had the tact to explain to me that these farewells were certainly temporary, since it was very likely that he would travel someday through France.

Viaticum

Amman, August 15, 2001

Our plane was scheduled to take off at eight o'clock in the morning; therefore we had to be at the airport in Amman at six o'clock. The previous evening I asked our taxi to come to Zarqa much earlier than necessary: at three o'clock.

At four in the morning, while the night was still dark, I rang at the residence of Monsignor Rabah. I was a little sleepy but rejoiced in advance over the surprise that I had for him. He came personally to open the door, a smile on his lips. I was sure that I was not disturbing his sleep, because generally he arose very early: it was the only time when he could have a bit of quiet for his prayer. But I had not expected that he himself would come to open the door for me!

"When I heard the doorbell, I wondered whether it was you", he explained.

Here then was the reason for that strange coincidence: I had been present in his thoughts and his prayer, almost as though he had been waiting for me. I presented to him my extraordinary request, which I had been pondering since the previous evening: "I would like you to say Mass for us before we leave."

In view of the dangers that certainly awaited us at the airport, it was better to take a substantial viaticum, provisions for the journey. It was not written in stone that we would see the end of that day.

Monsignor Rabah gestured to us to enter and led us to the chapel as though that were the most natural thing in the world to do. We remained in silence for several minutes while he vested in his alb and chasuble. Then he bowed profoundly before the little altar before kissing it respectfully.

At the end of the Mass I remained for a moment alone in front of the tabernacle. Once again the "Bread of Life" received from the hands of a priest had obtained peace of mind for me. During the whole first part of the ceremony, however, I had been constantly examining the bleakest scenarios for the hours to come.

From now on I kept fear at bay, and I allowed a bit of room for confidence. Above all I had the feeling that this new departure was less tense than when we had left Iraq. That time the last few weeks had been terribly trying, because of the constant pressure that my family had been under.

Here there was nothing of the sort: the danger was more distant, less concrete. That had allowed us to live peacefully during those last days in Jordan. As I left the chapel, I was so serene that I kept in my hand the Gospel and a prayer book. I put them in my pocket, without thinking of the danger that they would pose for me at the airport: they were indisputable proof of my conversion.

My watch said five o'clock. Time was pressing. We had to leave, hoping that we would have enough spare time to go through the checkpoints at the airport.

Our farewells with Monsignor Rabah were brief but charged with emotion. At that precise moment, if I had had the choice to remain with him, I would have done so without hesitation. It was truly distressing now to leave him. At the same time, I felt an almost physical relief in delivering our friends—Monsignor Rabah, Sister Maryam, Oum Farah—from the constant danger that helping a Muslim convert meant for them. I was well aware of having been a burden to them, and that added guilt to my burden.

Once we had arrived at the airport, we stayed in the taxi and waited for Sister Maryam. She left to look for the two Jordanian agents who were to guarantee our safety at the moment of our departure.

The minutes went by, interminably. Each one increased my tension. My imagination ran wild: wasn't all this agitation about an airplane just a bad dream? All at once I began to hope that that was the case, so as to avoid the horrors of going through customs. That was what I feared most.

Suddenly the door opened. Sister Maryam was alone. Before she had said a word I already knew that there was a problem.

"No sign of the agents", she blurted, vexed.

"Well? What do we do?"

I had the impression of being a little child who looks fearfully at his mother. But the hour was drawing near, and we had to make a decision.

"You will go anyway!" the nun finally declared, in a tone that allowed no contradiction.

Following her lead, we got out of the car, loaded down with our baggage, and walked toward the counter to register. There the employee carefully looked at the tickets presented by Sister Maryam; he looked for a moment at the passports, then went back to the tickets.

"I'll be right back", he said to us with a fleeting glance.

He had left with our passports. I did not like that at all—the absence of the agents who were supposed to guide us past barriers, and now the punctiliousness of the clerk at the counter. We waited for a good ten minutes. When he returned we were hanging on his every word, hoping for the words that would open to us our first door toward freedom.

"There is no return trip planned?" he asked.

"No ...", I replied, a bit hesitant as to the answer that I should give.

"I have to have the return tickets, or else you cannot board the plane."

That was final—and demoralizing.

"But they can buy them right here."

"I have to have the return tickets", the employee repeated with an evident lack of goodwill.

Turning away from the employee, the nun walked with measured steps toward the travel agency situated a little farther on. The information was not reassuring: we would have to pay seven hundred dinars per person for the return tickets, which was a considerable sum for the four of us. That was more than three times the price of the flight to France.

I rejected that option.

"That is impossible, Sister Maryam; seven hundred dinars is extravagantly expensive!"

I then turned toward the clerk, assuming my most piteous tone to gain his sympathy:

"Do you realize, seven hundred dinars is too expensive for us; we can't pay it."

"I don't care. If you do not have return tickets, you cannot depart!"

Determined, Sister Maryam did not intend to let a question of money stop her. Having decided to acquire the said tickets, she did not leave me any choice and walked again toward the agency. I could not help admiring her devotion.

Meanwhile the travel agency office had closed. We were now at an impasse. More unsettling was the fact that I had not seen our passports again since handing them over. After examining them in the back office, the employee had kept them with him. Sometimes he held them in his hand while speaking to us, without any sign that he was about to return them to us.

Almost an hour had passed since our arrival at the counter. I was on the verge of giving up, but Sister Maryam did not seem ready to put down her weapons.

Given the energy displayed by the nun, who pretended that she was going to debate the matter once more and besiege his counter until winning her case, the battle-weary employee agreed to reconsider his position, no doubt aware that he had overstepped his authority. He looked at our tickets again to see whether there might not actually be another solution.

The examination proceeded slowly, very slowly. My stomach churned while enduring that torment. Finally the man at the counter looked up at us and, smiling with a hint of condescension, started to register our baggage.

I breathed again and at the same time was enraged at that obscure clerk. Who had given him that discretionary power over us? Whose orders was he obeying to prevent us at all costs from boarding the airplane?

"Go ahead", he finally said to us, pointing toward the office of fines. That is where every Iraqi refugee has to appear before departing from Jordan, to verify that his situation is in order. All those who have stayed in the territory illegally have to pay a penalty: one and a half dinars per day. If the fine is not paid, the government marks the passport with a five-year prohibition against staying in Jordan. For me that would be a lesser evil, because the bill was [not as] steep: it amounted to twelve hundred dinars.

It seemed that in that airport I was doomed to undergo special treatment. In my case, the official explained to me that the second solution—banishment—was out of the question, for an obscure reason that I had to accept without discussion.

Obviously no one was fooled, but we had no choice—especially since the clerk seemed to take malicious pleasure in raising the bid. He too took our passports and disappeared into the back office for a long while. I wiped my forehead, which was soaked with perspiration, while Sister Maryam stamped her foot.

This again confirmed the hypothesis that someone was trying at all costs to keep me there. But who? The French embassy, however, had intervened to allow me to leave.

Sister Maryam, to whom I mentioned my anxieties, leaned toward resisting on principle the lowest machinations of the Jordanian government—one more sign that Christians were rejected.

The clerk finally came back toward us, looked suspiciously at the nun, and finally blurted out: "And who are you? What is your connection with this family? And why are you interfering?"

"I am a friend, and if you continue you will make my blood pressure rise! You know, when your blood pressure rises, it can be dangerous to your health. Now, will you give us these passports?"

"That will be one thousand two hundred dinars!"

After Sister Maryam gave him the money, the customs agent nevertheless kept the passports in his hand, as though he had no intention whatsoever of giving them back to us, as though he wanted to delay us as much as possible and do everything in his power to make us miss the plane.

It was the most trying day of my life. I could not bear any more of that tension. I was ready to abandon everything, to turn back so as to put an end to those psychological strong-arm tactics, since I did not see how we could emerge victorious.

Fortunately, Sister Maryam stood firm. She looked the agent right in the eye, determined to get our passports, and finally she prevailed!

Overcome by a veiled woman, the employee disdainfully handed us our papers, and we rushed toward the boarding area, hoping that the plane had waited for us. Out of breath, I glanced anxiously at the airport clock, which showed half past eight!

I stopped short and my arms went limp. I did not even know why I was running, since the plane had already taken off. We were lost.

Sister Maryam had turned around; she was desolate and looked at me as if to say, "I did all that I could." Suddenly a voice resounded over the loudspeaker: "Muhammad Fadel Ali, the flight to Paris is waiting, gate number 7."

It was hard to believe. Certainly I had been spared nothing, to the last moment. When I was convinced that everything was ruined, the situation was resolved, as though by a miracle.

"French, the Language of God"

Flight from Amman to Paris, August 15, 2001

It was the first time that I had taken an airplane. After settling my wife and children, I ended up finding a seat—beside a Syrian priest! I smiled at this new wink [from heaven]; I saw in it a good omen for what awaited us in Europe.

Nevertheless I asked him to pray for us, hinting at how difficult this departure was, being uprooted from my family, from my country, uprooted from my friends in Jordan.

And I would also need a lot of courage to rebuild my life in an unknown world. From now on I would no longer be called Youssef but Joseph, which apparently sounds more French.

Over there in Europe I had neither address nor telephone number, only one contact with a Frenchman, Thierry, an agricultural engineer in Jordan. He was the one who had agreed to organize our arrival in France, to vouch for us at the embassy. His parents had consented to be our host family.

Since he worked alongside Palestinians, the Frenchman preferred to take another plane, two days earlier, so as not to compromise himself by openly helping a Christian, and also to prepare for our coming. In the haste of our departure, we agreed that Sister Maryam would be the one to inform him of our time of arrival.

During the eight-hour flight I saw my life, the one that I was leaving behind, pass before my eyes in fast motion. Without the hand of God, I would never have come through that adventure alive. That providential force had kept my wife quiet, preventing her from denouncing me to her family; it had also caused a seven-year-old child, Sayid's son, to deny that he knew my son Azhar; this force had also enabled us to escape the police in Karak, thanks to the presence of Oum Farah. And finally, the most incredible thing was that the bullet shot by my uncle at point-blank range had not hit me. These reflections made me quite serious: what plan

did heaven have in store for us in the future, that we had
been so highly favored?

Upon our arrival at Paris-Orly Airport, after going through
customs, I noticed the Frenchman who was waiting for us,
all smiles that he had not missed us. Indeed, he explained
to me that Sister Maryam had not notified him as we had
agreed. I frowned, worried by that news. What had happened to her? I was already imagining the worst, filled with
remorse at the thought of having endangered the life of the
nun. But Thierry did not want us to be alarmed without
knowing. He brought us to his parents' residence in Paris
so as to drop off our bags.

In the car I was quite surprised by the colors of the country, first by that of the trees along the highway; their saturated green seemed almost artificial to me. In my country
and even in Jordan, the sun and its rays are extremely strong,
overwhelmingly so; in contrast all the other colors become
dull and grayish. Even the architecture had yielded to this
phenomenon. Here, on the contrary, the colors leaped out
at me with their nuances and variety. I was also surprised
to see sloping roofs, and the cut stone of Parisian buildings;
back home, the houses are flat and unattractive, built of
concrete blocks that are often visible.

Thierry's parents offered us tea, and their welcome gave
me a moment's respite. Ever since our arrival I had not
stopped watching for the moment when agents would come
to arrest us. I still remembered the very precise words of
the French consul in Amman: "Your names have been posted
by the police." I was convinced that this surveillance had
pursued us all the way here.

The fact that there was no news about Sister Maryam
reinforced this conviction. Although Thierry made several calls,
no one seemed to know what had happened to the nun.

Despite my fears, Thierry insisted, with his few words of Arabic, that we should go out. He wanted to take us immediately to Notre Dame Cathedral because, he said, it was August 15. In his opinion we should not miss the beautiful feast of the Assumption.

"We already went to Mass, very early this morning", I explained to him, before telling him about that unique moment with Monsignor Rabah.

"Yes, but here there is a procession", he replied. We were in France, in a country where Christians are free to have processions.

It would take time, however, for us to be free at last from fear, that second skin that had constantly been with us for so many years. Yet the first days in this country had given me several encouraging signs. First of all, Marie and I were very moved by the family that welcomed us warmly and so considerately, without expecting anything in return. It reminded me of the welcome that we had received at the home of Oum Farah, in Fuheis.

The day after our arrival, Thierry finally relayed to me good news about Sister Maryam, when we were worried sick. While leaving the airport she had been accosted by two policemen who asked her what her connection with me was. She replied that she had "seen the woman crying, that's all".

So as to be prudent, she had not gone directly back to her community. She left for the South, toward Kerak. After a while her pursuers stopped tailing her, and she was finally able to stop at the side of the road, where she immediately fell asleep, one hand on the steering wheel, the other on her portable phone, which she had turned on.

This good news set my mind a little more at ease so that I could take an interest in the customs of this country, especially the religious practices. And so, on the following Sunday, Thierry brought us to the church of Val-de-Grâce, where he sang Gregorian chant with the choir.

I was gripped by the sonorities, which were much subtler and musical than Arabic. Although I did not understand it, I immediately felt an attraction for that language.

As I listened to that slow, profound music, I also found again the prayerful atmosphere that I had experienced in churches in the Near East. This chant touched me deeply; it immersed me in a peace that I could not have imagined only a few days before.

What impressed me most was the silence that set in after the psalmody; it was tangible, and to me it seemed filled with the divine presence. As we left the church, I told Thierry, "Those chants are really very beautiful! It is as though French were the language of God."

"That was not French, but Latin", Thierry replied with a smile.

The name didn't matter, since I knew nothing more about it. For me, it was the language of the Latin Church of the West. Yet oddly enough, I found in it a bit of my faith, which had been born in a land of the East.

EPILOGUE

One month after my arrival in France, my father died. I learned about it only two years later, from an Iraqi friend with whom I have stayed in contact.

Several months later I had a conversation on the telephone with my brother Hussein, one of the ones who had shot at me. Despite everything, I still had some affection for him.

We never talk about that attempt on my life; that would be beyond my strength. We are aware that there is too great a risk of breaking the slender thread that still connects us. A frank explanation would release too much emotion for that fragile relation with my family to bear.

So as not to open up the dikes of anger, we strictly limit ourselves to exchanging news, and that is not so bad. Sometimes I even sense in him a desire to help me, to get me out of the poverty in which I live in France; for it is true that we are living today on the public generosity of that country, after having slowly exhausted our funds.

"Come back to Iraq", my brother Hussein suggested to me. "I will have a house built for you far from Baghdad."

That touches me. I can tell that it is my father who is expressing, posthumously, the desire to see me return to his country and be close to his family. But I don't have the trust.

Through oblique remarks that Hussein makes, I sense that my mother has not pardoned me. As she sees it, I am responsible for my father's death. During his agony he was still calling, "Muhammad ... Where is Muhammad? I know that he is not dead!"

I weep every time that I think of it. It is painful for me not to have been able to explain my new life, which was so distant from his own world.

In retrospect it seems to me that he intended to subject me to a sort of electroshock treatment, by the prison, then the fatwa, so as to make me forget my conversion to Christ. But he never wanted my death or a definitive separation.

I don't know why, but the thought consoles me a little. Maybe it is because it makes me hope that between us, beyond our radically divergent paths, there is still some remnant of affection and mutual esteem. That diminishes my homesickness and the pain of estrangement.

Here in France we are gradually regaining a certain sense of security, as well as relative peace of mind. The fear in Anwar's heart and in mine has calmed; the wounds are becoming less painful.

My wife, who is still very sensitive to poetry and symbols, sees a sign of divine solicitude in the present of a rare bird that came to perch on her windowsill on the eve of our departure from Jordan. She saw it again in Paris, just before we moved to a larger apartment. She has looked for the name of this beautiful bird with unique colors in dictionaries and books about wildlife, but has never found it.

I still have one step to take.

It will take time, a lot of time, for me to forgive my family for all that they made me suffer: prison, torture, lack of money. How many times I told myself, with each new trial, that it was all their fault.

It was not because of Christ that I suffered, but because of the lack of freedom imposed by Muslim society, which my family did not dare to give up, because of pride and their concern for respectability.

On the other hand, Christ is the one who helped me to get through those difficulties. During all those years, not one day did his love for me fail. He it was who gave me the courage and the patience to keep going, without despairing.

In the midst of the persecutions that have assailed me, I was even proud to have been able to witness to my Christian faith, especially at the time of the attempt on my life. I tried at least to show my brothers the emptiness of their belief.

I am thinking in particular of one of my four brothers who were present that day, Haïdar/Hayidar. Since that discussion between us and the violence that ensued, he lost his Muslim faith and now lives as an atheist. I think about him every day, as I do about all my relatives who continue to live in the darkness of Islam, like the sons of my uncle Karim, who have become turban-wearing imams.

How I hope that they will know the light of Christ, but without the horrors that I have experienced. I learned since my arrival in France that I am not the only convert in Iraq: others have followed the same path as I did, all of them clandestinely because they are persecuted. I wish that someday the whole Musawi clan could convert. For that to happen, society itself would have to change, along with its laws, but alas, Islam has bolted the door against it.

Meanwhile my family is indeed the cause of all my troubles. And that is the hardest thing for me to accept.

I fight every day, though, against that bitterness, knowing very well that it is not Christian. Of all the battles that I have fought until now, this will certainly be the most difficult. I have asked friends and priests whom I have met to pray for me, that I may truly find the will to forgive.

In a certain sense imprisonment had a beneficial effect also: it made me reflect about myself and the violence that is deep inside me. Without that opportunity, I could very well have reacted brutally to my family's behavior; I was even ready to kill them. When I left prison, though, that had become something impossible for me: prayer and reflection had made me understand that I could no longer conduct myself like a non-Christian.

This, no doubt, is the most difficult thing that Christ is asking of me today: to love my enemies. That may seem easy when you don't have any. But when you have opponents, persons who have left marks in your flesh, then that is the real test of authenticity for the believer, the test that shows whether you are really Christian.

The awareness that I still have that hatred in me is truly painful, a thorn in my faith. But I consider it well worth it, now that I belong to the religion that I freely chose to embrace.

For this religion I have already abandoned much of myself. I used to tell myself that I deserved to be baptized, because I had paid the price, and very dearly. If I am a Christian today, it is not because I inherited it from my parents.

From now on, if I want to attain complete union with Christ—I now know that he was the one whom I glimpsed that memorable night sixteen years ago—I have to take one step further, no doubt the most costly step, because it is against myself that I must fight.